A GUIDE TO HEMINGWAY'S
KEY WEST

A Guide to

HEMINGWAY'S
KEY WEST

MARK ALLEN BAKER

THE
History
PRESS

Published by The History Press
Charleston, SC
www.historypress.com

Front cover, bottom: Ernest Hemingway's home in Key West, Florida. P*hoto by Carol Highsmith, Library of Congres*; *top, left to right*: Hemingway in uniform, 1918. *Ernest Hemingway Collection. John F. Kennedy Presidential Library and Museum, Boston*; Hemingway's writing studio; and Hemingway posing with a marlin. *Ernest Hemingway Collection. John F. Kennedy Presidential Library and Museum, Boston. Back cover, top*: Ernest Hemingway sitting by the pool at Finca Vigía, San Francisco de Paula, Cuba. *Ernest Hemingway Collection. John F. Kennedy Presidential Library and Museum, Boston*; *inset*: Joe Russell's Sloppy Joe's bar, where Hemingway and his Mob caroused.

All images without a source reference are courtesy of the author.

First published 2022

Manufactured in the United States

ISBN 9781467151023

Library of Congress Control Number: 2022930154

In loving memory of:

Nancy L. Allen (February 13, 1941–November 6, 2019) and Thomas Patrick Allen (May 25, 1961–July 12, 2021).

CONTENTS

PREFACE

D iscover a century of island magnetism by walking in the footsteps of a literary legend. The centennial of Ernest Hemingway's initial visit to Key West is approaching, so it is not a surprise that most visitors, along with island residents, find themselves reflecting on the life of the famous author. For a dozen years (1928 until 1940), the resident wordsmith produced a consistent stream of quality work. And in so doing, Hemingway solidified his reputation as one of the finest writers of the twentieth century. Arguably, these were the most important years of his life; the Hemingway Myth was born, refined and polished in Key West. In retrospect, it redefined the island culture while guaranteeing the author's immortality.

Why Key West? What made this juncture in the author's life so meaningful? Was it the weather? Was it the recreation? Or was it the camaraderie? Understanding that creativity, not to mention productivity, required certain elements—components that are unique to each individual—I sought those secrets.

My first visit to Key West took place in 1959, a couple years before the author's tragic suicide. Too young to realize who Ernest Hemingway was, I nevertheless remembered the name. Haunted by Hemingway ever since, I have found the association both enlightening and peculiar. Enlightening, in that I find the man fascinating as a subject, peculiar in that it took so long to determine why (see chapter 8).

Likely taken around 1900, this is a hotel view looking west toward the Gulf of Mexico. *Library of Congress, LC-DIG-det-4a28948 (digital file from b&w glass transparency).*

Over the years, I was drawn to everything about the man, prompting me to accumulate every reference to his life, from first-edition books and original magazine articles to telegrams he sent and checks he cashed. When an important artifact of his life surfaced in the auction market, I couldn't resist a purchase. I corresponded with his friends, such as A.E. Hotchner, and biographers, like Carlos Baker. Speaking at the Hemingway Days Festival about my passion for the writer allowed me to meet members of his family. I even turned down a lunch invitation from some of the finest university scholars in order to grab a bite to eat with Hemingway's last living sparring partners—the sweet science never far from my life.

Throughout this journey, I always sought a book that I could never find. A book that would allow me to walk in his footsteps. A book that would assist me in discovering answers to my questions. What did Hemingway see, hear, feel and touch when he lived in Key West? What places did he frequent, and where were they located? Who were the members of the Hemingway Mob, and what were they like? Where did they live? What places did they frequent? In essence: What was left of the Hemingway island mystique?

Much has changed in Key West over the past century. Buildings have been torn down or replaced. Businesses fluctuated with the economic conditions, leaving some to prosper and others to fail. And property once public may now be private. Mindful of all these factors, and respectful of personal property, I spent thousands of hours researching and recreating the author's footsteps. And from it, I had a better sense of his life on the island.

Join me on three sojourns, or tours—designed for your convenience and adaptable to your lifestyle and mode of transportation—as we walk in the footsteps of Ernest Hemingway.

ACKNOWLEDGEMENTS

"Cultivate the habit of being grateful for every good thing that comes to you, and to give thanks continuously. And because all things have contributed to your advancement, you should include all things in your gratitude." Emerson said it, and I live by it. As this is my seventh book for The History Press/Arcadia Publishing, I wish to extend my gratitude to the entire production team, which always does a magnificent job preparing a title. Also, I wish to extend my appreciation to Joe Gartrell, Michael G. Kinsella, Caitlyn Post, Crystal Murray, Abigail Fleming and Dani McGrath.

As with my previous titles, I have had the opportunity to work with outstanding institutions, including Key West Chamber of Commerce, the John F. Kennedy Presidential Library and Museum, the Library of Congress, the National Archives and Records Administration, State Archives of Florida, United States Department of State–Bureau of Consular Affairs, Federal Bureau of Investigation and the Hemingway House and Museum. As this work encompasses years of research, I owe a special note of recognition to Carlos Baker, Kermit "Shine" Forbes, A.E. Hotchner, James "Iron Baby" Roberts, Tony Tarracino and many others associated with the author.

As always, my love to my friends and family, especially my wife, Alison.

Introduction

HEMINGWAY ON BOXING

Boxing has always been a metaphor for life, and always will be because it is an individual sport that pits man against man, in "mano a mano" (or "hand to hand") combat. While the latter term originated from bullfighting and was used to describe a duel between two matadors, hand-to-hand combat existed before man decided to subdue, immobilize and then kill a bull.[1] It existed before man could even communicate. As the oldest of all sports, boxing dates to 1500 BC. If fist fighting was good enough for the gods on Olympus, then it was good enough for the Greeks.

Writers love the sport because of the idioms it produces, like "on the ropes," "roll with the punches," "down but not out" and "puncher's chance," to name a few. Ernest Miller Hemingway loved the fight game, or *sweet science*. He followed certain fighters and even penned a boxing story for the April 1916 edition of *Tabula*, Oak Park High School's literary magazine.[2] As the sport grew in popularity, particularly during the late nineteenth and early twentieth centuries, so too did the frequency of stories. George Bernard Shaw penned *Cashel Byron's Profession* in 1882, Jack London's "A Piece of Steak" was published in the *Saturday Evening Post* in November 1909 and Sir Arthur Conan Doyle wrote several stories about boxing and even made Sherlock Holmes an amateur boxer.

Hemingway delighted that there was a hierarchy to boxing—contenders battled one another in hopes of vying for a title or championship. To him such a scale existed in writing as well. As a consummate competitor, he discussed writers he would like to defeat. Since the *New York Times* bestseller list was first published on October 12, 1931— a mere seven years after *The Ring* began publishing annual ratings of boxers, I might add—he knew where he stood. Like a fighter climbing the rankings of his weight class, the author perceived each book release as a victory over another contender. Believing that he was destined to be champion, he yearned for the title. Once had, he planned on keeping it.

"The Battler" was an early Hemingway short story that found its way into *In Our Time* (1925), published by Boni & Liveright. It features Nick Adams, or the author's autobiographical alter ego. Caught as a stowaway, Adams is thrown from a train. He then encounters Ad Francis, a former boxing champion. Admitting he has experienced cognitive issues as a result of boxing, Francis eventually ignites an altercation with Adams.[3] It is likely that Ad Francis is patterned after Ad Wolgast, aka "Michigan Wildcat," former world's lightweight champion (1910–1912). Wolgast, who took terrible beatings in the ring, suffered from the same issues as Ad Francis and was eventually committed to Stockton State Hospital.

A character in *The Sun Also Rises* (1926), Robert Cohn, is a Jewish boxer from a wealthy New York family.[4] And he is not the type of pugilist most would imagine. While attending Princeton, Cohn uses the sport as a vehicle to counter his shyness and feelings of inferiority.[5] Seeking love and acceptance, his sacrifice comes in the form of training in the gym and suffering in the ring. As the only Jew and nonveteran among his friends, Cohn becomes a target for their insecurities. Since he did not participate in World War I, Cohn holds on to traditional values and beliefs that the others have lost. The postwar world had changed, and Robert Cohn's behavior, contrasted against his friends, is proof.[6]

Having completed and mailed off *The Sun Also Rises*, Ernest Hemingway finally had an opportunity to pen a few short stories, one of which was "Fifty Grand." The story illustrates the author's love and command of the sport. It follows aging champion Jack Brennan as he prepares himself for a battle against challenger Jimmy Walcott. Gambling, forever a factor in boxing, enters the picture to undermine Brennan's integrity. The scenario, all too familiar with those who follow the sport today, was unique when it was first published in the *Atlantic Monthly* in July 1927 and later the same year in the author's book *Men Without Women*.

Dissected from every point of view by literary critics, the story remains classic Hemingway for its subject matter and presentation—the reader is forced to draw their own conclusion as to why Jack Brennan places his

$50,000 wager.[7] Analysis of omitted pages from the original manuscript support that the fight was likely based on the Jack Britton (aging champion) versus Mickey Walker (challenger and rising star) fight held at Madison Square Garden on November 1, 1922, with inspiration provided from Battling Siki's sixth-round knockout of Georges Carpentier during a battle held in France on September 24, 1922. Initially, the referee disqualified Siki for tripping Carpentier, only to be overruled by ringside officials. Understanding conflict from every angle, Hemingway's depth of knowledge even played into his depiction of Jack Brennan's training. Brennan, the current welterweight champion, goes to a "health farm," Danny Hogan's New Jersey training camp. To little surprise, Hogan's facility resembles Madam Bey's internationally known training camp located at 516 River Road in Chatham Township, New Jersey.

Penned the same year, "The Killers" is a short story—one of the first boxing pieces to examine the relationship between boxing and organized crime—that appeared first in *Scribner's Magazine* before being published in *Men Without Women*.[8] Nick Adams is featured in a struggle to understand the contrast between power and powerlessness. He witnesses two hit men entering a restaurant to kill a Swedish boxer by the name of Ole Andreson. To add a bit of historical context: Not long before Hemingway put pen to paper, the Chicago mob transferred its operations to the suburb of Summit, where "The Killers" is set. Organized crime also ordered the killing of a popular heavyweight boxer named Andre Anderson. Even if the boxer was known for knocking down and drawing Jack Dempsey on June 24, 1916, Anderson was believed to be a fighter who cooperated with underworld figures. He was shot and killed following an argument in a Cicero, Illinois soda fountain.[9]

As a youngster, Hemingway dreamed about being a prizefighter. From mimicking the poses of heavyweight greats to transforming his mother's music room into a gymnasium, there were times when the dream didn't seem that far off. He sparred with a few of his friends and acquaintances in Paris, including Harold Loeb, George O'Neil and Paul Fisher, and attended prizefights at the Cirque de Paris. And it was there that he even befriended Larry Gains, the talented Black heavyweight.[10]

When the author, not yet thirty years old, strolled into the island paradise of Key West, he was a stranger—likely another rumrunner, some thought. Despite the fact that Hemingway had published a number of works, including the internationally acclaimed novel *The Sun Also Rises*, nobody knew who he was.[11] While the lack of recognition bothered him, that would soon change when the local bookstore began stocking his work. Hemingway enjoyed the challenge of proving himself on the island and, if necessary, off. Doing so inside a pair of boxing mitts was one option—behind a rod and reel, he believed, was another.

When the author discovered that there was boxing at the Key West Arena, at the northeast corner of Thomas and Petronia Streets, he lit up like a lightbulb. That was a good thing, as the poorly lit makeshift ring needed all the illumination it could get. All kidding aside, Depression-era boxing was cheap entertainment. Friday night was fight night, and $1.25 could get a fight fan general admission to the grandstand, and $3.00 could grab a seat ringside. Fighters, primarily island boxers, received a cut of the gate, which could be a week's pay if the event drew a few hundred spectators.

Evenings at the arena could be chaotic, but they were also entertaining thanks to exciting local talent. Noteworthy boxers included Alfred "Black Pie" Colebrooks, Kermit "Shine" (aka "Battling Geech") Forbes, Victor Laurie, Joe Mills, James "Iron Baby" Roberts and Larry Samber. As a frequent spectator, Ernest Hemingway familiarized himself with the skills of each and even picked up a few dollars thanks to solid wagers. And it wasn't long before he landed himself the best view in the house: As referee, or the third man in the ring, he understood the rules and didn't hesitate to enforce them.

Kermit Forbes often spoke of his initial meeting with the author. During a fight between Joe Mills and Alfred Colebrooks, the latter initiated a low blow that prompted referee Hemingway to eject Colebrooks from the ring and award the fight to Mills. Forbes, who was a good friend of Colebrooks, was furious over the judgment and leaped into the ring to take matters, or the referee, into his own hands. Grabbing Hemingway by the ears, Forbes wrestled the author to the floor. Shocked by the action, Hemingway gained his control and flung the much smaller Forbes into the center of the ring. Bystanders quickly separated the pair, as both disheveled combatants attempted to regain their composure. Later, Forbes, who had no idea the true identity of the arbiter, went to the author's home at 907 Whitehead Street to apologize. Hemingway, aware of who Forbes was, accepted the apology, and the pair became friends and even sparring partners.

It wasn't long after the purchase of Hemingway's now famous residence that the author had a backyard ring set up. Forbes claimed it was located where the pool was installed. (Perhaps Pauline was making a statement with regard to her husband's form of recreation. More on that later.) As Hemingway paid fifty cents a round, word traveled fast among island pugilists. And it wasn't long before the aforementioned island boxers found themselves routinely sparring with Mr. Ernest.[12] (By the way, Hemingway wore headgear; his sparring partners did not.)

The author had a variety of training materials, including two speed bags, a heavy bag, and numerous pairs of gloves (eight, ten and sixteen ounces). The intent was always to spar and conduct an injury-free workout. Asked if the author ever pulled any of his punches, Forbes said he didn't believe he did. Hemingway liked the action and urged Forbes to turn his punches loose. Was Hemingway a good boxer? Forbes, who chuckled when asked, affirmed that it didn't matter at fifty cents a round.[13]

Novelist Morley Callaghan, who sparred with Hemingway, believed they were both amateurs in a man's sport. Hemingway was attracted to the dramatic element—over technique and dedication—of the sport. Callaghan, favoring the latter, assessed his sparring partner as nothing more than target practice. The great Jack Dempsey, who had an opportunity to spar with anyone he wanted in Paris during the 1920s, read Hemingway like a book. Although the author was in shape, Dempsey could sense his unpredictability and refused to spar with him. He was the sort of fellow, the heavyweight champion believed, whom he would have to injure in order to make a statement. "The Manassa Mauler" didn't want to do that.

Gene Tunney, a heavyweight champion and friend of the author, agreed with Dempsey's assessment. Nevertheless, Tunney entered a boxing ring to spar with Hemingway. True to Dempsey's appraisal, when the author tossed an overly aggressive right hand, Tunney unleashed a powerful right of his own that stopped a fingernail length from beheading the cocksure wordsmith. An inch from dreamland, Hemingway got the picture.

Boxing, a key element in support of his manhood, was one of many threads—hunting, fishing and bullfighting, among others—that ran through the life and work of Ernest Miller Hemingway. And because it did, the male protagonists in many of his stories share his machismo. Exhibiting grace under fire, they all possess a part of the soul of their creator. It was the Heming Way, or the courage to live with the absence of antipathy.

ERNEST HEMINGWAY'S KEY WEST
(1928-1940)

'm sitting on top of the world," Al Jolson crooned, and why not? People were happy: Calvin Coolidge, a Republican lawyer from New England, was carrying us down the road to prosperity, and land on Broadway and Wall Street in New York City was selling at a record price. Life was grand. Described on his passport as "6 feet tall, pointed chin, medium forehead, dark brown hair, brown eyes, fair complexion, straight nose and oval face," Ernest Miller Hemingway, age twenty-six, appeared to be on the cusp of literary success. He need only make a couple decisive decisions to ensure his destiny.

ERNEST HEMINGWAY WAS BORN on July 21, 1889, in the affluent Chicago suburb of Oak Park, Illinois. His father, Clarence Edmonds Hemingway, was a physician, and his mother, Grace Hall Hemingway, a musician. As the dominant figure in the family, Grace ruled the roost, as they say. Named after his grandfather, Ernest Miller Hall, young Ernest was the first son and the second of the Hemingways' six children. Talented both in and out of the classroom, Ernest appeared destined to become a good writer or athlete or perhaps even an outdoorsman, as he loved to hunt and fish. After leaving high school—he did not attend college—Hemingway became a cub reporter for the *Kansas City Star*. And it was there that he skillfully utilized "The Star Copy Style," a guide that would form the foundation for his prose.[14]

The changing landscape in Europe brought about World War I. And when his country called, Ernest Hemingway answered. Although he was rejected by the U.S. Army for poor eyesight, he signed on with the Red Cross as an ambulance driver in Italy. Wounded by mortar fire, he spent his recuperation in a Red Cross hospital in Milan. It was while convalescing that he fell in love with a tall, bright-eyed Red Cross nurse named Agnes von Kurowsky. Seven years older than her teenage admirer, she was flattered by his affections. When Hemingway returned to the United States in January 1919, he believed he was destined to marry Agnes. He was wrong.

In December 1917, after being rejected by the U.S. Army for poor eyesight, Ernest Hemingway responded to a Red Cross recruitment effort and signed on to be an ambulance driver in Italy. His uniform was on display at the Key West Art and Historical Society.

Upon receiving a "Dear Ernest" letter from Agnes in March 1919, the myth of living happily ever after died with the relationship. Complicating matters, the adjustment to civilian life presented a challenge. After a Michigan fishing and camping trip with his high school buddies, Hemingway was offered a job in Toronto—courtesy of a family friend. He accepted, and it led to a position as a freelancer and staff writer for the *Toronto Star Weekly*. Returning to Michigan briefly, he moved next to Chicago in September 1920. While living there with friends, he took a job as an associate editor of the monthly journal *Cooperative Commonwealth*.

Even if he wasn't looking for love, especially after his relationship with Agnes, Hemingway wasn't blind to the idea. When the beautiful red-haired sister of his Chicago roommate paid a visit, the thought took on a face. Eight years older than Hemingway, Hadley Richardson had briefly attended college before returning home to St. Louis to care for her mother.[15] Her devotion to family and sense of responsibility impressed many, including the young journal editor. After corresponding for months, the pair married on September 3, 1921, in Bay Township, Michigan.

Upon the advice of novelist Sherwood Anderson, whom Hemingway met in Chicago, the pair headed for Paris. And it would be through Anderson that Hemingway was given introductions to the Parisian literary set: John Dos Passos, F. Scott Fitzgerald, Ford Madox Ford, James Joyce, Ezra Pound,

Ernest Hemingway's wallet, calling card and photograph. These items were on display at The Key West Art & Historical Society.

Gertrude Stein and Alice B. Toklas. Having accepted a job as a foreign correspondent for the *Toronto Star*, Ernest, accompanied by his bride, soon fell into a comfortable yet economical lifestyle in Europe.

The only child of Ernest and Hadley Hemingway, John Hadley Nicanor Hemingway, was born on October 10, 1923, in Toronto, Ontario, Canada. "Bumby," as he was nicknamed—he had Gertrude Stein and Alice B. Toklas as his godparents—appeared destined for a literary life.

Ernest Hemingway, Elizabeth Hadley Richardson and Jack "Bumby" Hemingway, Schruns, Austria, spring 1926. *Ernest Hemingway Collection. John F. Kennedy Presidential Library and Museum, Boston.*

Writing short stories to subsidize his income, Ernest Hemingway wasn't living a life of luxury, but he did manage to do a bit of traveling. Spain, and even Austria, provided new vistas for the family. Fascinated by bullfighting, Ernest was profoundly moved by the Fiesta de San Fermín in Pamplona, Spain. It even became the setting for his novel *The Sun Also Rises*.

Enter Pauline Marie Pfeiffer, born on July 22, 1895, in Parkersburg, Iowa. Her affluent parents, Paul and Mary Pfeiffer, were attentive to their daughter's needs and committed to her education. Having moved to St. Louis in 1901, Pauline attended school at Visitation Academy of St. Louis. When her family moved to Piggott, Arkansas, she opted to stay in Missouri and study at the University of Missouri School of Journalism. Upon Pauline's graduation in 1918, she honed her skills at newspapers in Cleveland and New York before turning to magazine work. And it was in Paris, in 1926, while working for *Vogue*, that she met Ernest and Hadley Hemingway.

Back to the two decisions facing Hemingway early in 1926. The aspiring author had to choose between two publishers, Boni & Liveright, which published his first book, *In Our Time*, as part of a three-book contract, or Scribner's, a publishing firm with greater potential offering a long-term contract. The latter was the choice—the decision made easier when Boni & Liveright terminated Hemingway's contract.[16] Having begun an affair with Pauline Pfeiffer in February 1926, Hemingway's next decision was far more difficult: Ernest divorced Hadley in January 1927 and married Pauline in May.

Pauline and Ernest spent their honeymoon in Le Grau-du-Roi in southern France. As part of their marriage agreement, Hemingway converted to Catholicism. When Pauline found out she was pregnant, she wanted to have the baby in America. Where, they weren't sure. On the recommendation of John Dos Passos, Ernest and Pauline left Paris for Key West in March 1928. Sailing from La Rochelle aboard the *Orita*, they headed first to Havana, then on to their Florida island destination.

Key West in 1928

Billing itself as "Nature's Ideal Spot" in the late 1920s, Key West—all 4.2 square miles of it—considered the weather its greatest asset. Granted, the tropical savanna climate was tough to ignore, as was the abundant sunshine, but it didn't take long before visitors discovered other benefits. As a two-season wet and dry climate—the period from November through April was normally sunny and dry, with only 25 percent of the annual rainfall occurring, while May through October brought the precipitation—it took time for visitors to get used to the heavy tropical downpours, followed by intense sunshine, but few seemed to mind. For mainland Floridians, where showers and thunderstorms occur in the afternoon, the switch to morning showers was their first adjustment. Folks liked the consistency in temperature, refreshing easterly trade wind and that the Florida Keys and Miami Beach are the only places within the contiguous United States to have never recorded a frost or freeze. Because the humidity was often over 70 percent, it was hard for natives to believe that the record high temperature was only 97°F (36°C) on July 19, 1880.[17]

During the late 1920s, Key West was selling itself as disease-free by virtue of the purifying effect of the sea breeze. The island was quick to note that during the flu epidemic of 1918, deaths there were proportionally smaller than those of any other city in the United States. Visitors could rest assured: Key West's climate was disease resistant.

The location of the island made it the gateway to Cuba, the West Indies and Central America. And it was the nearest United States port to the Panama Canal. Thanks to the Florida East Coast Railway—the Key West extension, linking together the chain of Florida Keys—traveling had never been easier.[18] With its natural deep harbor, Key West was capable of berthing the largest vessels either in the deeper outer harbor or the inner harbor.[19] It was a resource the United States military found difficult to ignore.

As for ferries and steamships: the former arrived daily, while the latter offered a convenient schedule. The P.&O. Steamship Company offered daily service between Key West and Havana with biweekly trips made between Tampa and the Island City. The 105-mile trip between Key West and Havana took about six hours. The company operated four passenger steamers (largest capacity 425 passengers): *Cuba*, *Governor Cobb*, *Miami* and *Northland*. Simplifying matters, the steamships and the Florida East Coast Railway used the same terminals.

The Mallory Steam Line, formed in 1860 by Charles Henry Mallory, offered freight and passenger service from New York, Key West and Galveston.[20] And the luxurious steamships offered four-day trips from New York to Key West. There is no better way to convey the luxury than a quick view of the dinner menu; for cocktails they had fresh shrimp, Bengal chutney, diced celery and assorted olives; French onion and hot or jellied

A view of the Bahia Honda Rail Bridge in the lower Florida Keys. It once connected Bahia Honda Key with the Spanish Harbor Key.

consommé for soups; for entrées fresh mackerel, curried lobster with rice and prime ribs of beef au jus; vegetable choices were broccoli, mashed turnips, boiled or snow potatoes and creamed spinach; and for dessert you could have charlotte russe, vanilla ice cream, wine jelly with whipped cream, Nabisco wafers or even cheddar or camembert cheese and crackers.

Speaking of transportation, negotiations were underway between the United States and Cuba for the possible establishment of air service between Key West and Havana—the trip was estimated to take seventy-five minutes.

The U.S. military viewed Key West as the "Gibraltar of America," and it was called on as needed. Planes and ships of all types frequented the military base. From an army barracks and naval base hospital to a marine hospital and submarine base, the versatility of the military was always on display.

The best cigars in the world, using Havana tobacco, were made in Key West. The similarity of the climates, not to mention ingredients, made it impossible to tell where the cigars were produced. As one of the main industries on the island, cigar making employed thousands of local workers. If you didn't know where an individual worked, it was a good bet that it had something to do with a cylinder of tobacco rolled in tobacco leaves for smoking.

Thousands of pounds of fish and shellfish were shipped all over the world from Key West. And the island had the only green turtle canning factory in the country. And if it wasn't seafood being shipped, it was likely sponges. When grass, wool and yellow sponges were discovered in these waters, customers finally found a buying alternative to the Mediterranean countries.

Above: Construction on the original Overseas Highway lasted through most of the mid-1920s. It officially opened for traffic on January 25, 1928, and many souvenirs, such as those pictured, commemorated the event. These items were on display at the Key West Art and Historical Society.

Left: Transforming the economic infrastructure of the town in the first half of the twentieth century, Norberg Thompson significantly influenced the development of Key West. As Thompson's businesses were located in the Historic Seaport District, this is where you will find this statue.

If visitors needed a place to bed down, there was a situation to fit their budget. From the Casa Marina, Hotel La Concha, Jefferson Hotel and the Overseas Hotel to the Island City Hotel and Panama Hotel, visitors had plenty of choices when it came to quality accommodations. Boardinghouses, such as the Watrous House and the O'Brien House, were also available.

For those planning on staying a bit longer: Monroe County, of which Key West was the county seat, offered outstanding public education. And residents had options. Private schools were also available on the island. They included Convent of Mary Immaculate and St. Joseph's College. The Methodists also had a strong presence in educating the Cuban poor.

Picking up a copy of the *Key West Citizen*, the island's daily newspaper, a visitor could read about the progress being made on the island. From public services to utilities, the tropical paradise was paving the way for the future. Or so they hoped.

This was the Key West Ernest and Pauline Hemingway discovered.

Just Visiting

From 1920 until 1930, Key West suffered the largest percentage loss (-31.6 percent) of population in its history. The primary factor for the decline was the postwar reduction in navy personnel. Upon the Hemingways' arrival in April 1928, roughly twelve thousand people occupied the economically depressed island.[21] Honestly, it didn't bother Ernest and Pauline Hemingway, who had no reference or long-term plans. They accepted it for the paradise it was. Prohibition, or the prevention by law of the manufacture and sale of alcohol—in the United States between 1920 and 1933—was at the height of its unpopularity, yet you wouldn't have known it in Key West. Spirits flowed freely, as did the definition of morality.

Pauline's rich uncle Gus had promised the newlyweds a belated wedding present.[22] However, that gift, in the form of a new yellow Ford (roadster) automobile, was delayed in shipment to Key West. Knowing that their stay would be brief, they took up residence at the three-story Trevor & Morris Building, located at 314 Simonton Street, above the Ford dealership.[23]

Since the location could be loud during the day, Ernest, as he did in Paris, put pen to paper early in the morning and saved his afternoons for entertainment and discovery—in this instance it was fishing for barracuda, jack, red snapper and tarpon—along with island exploration. It was a productive schedule that gave him time to decompress in the afternoon.

Built with bricks from Fort Taylor, the Trev-Mor Hotel (Casa Antigua), as it was once called, hosted Ernest Hemingway and his wife in 1928.

By April, he had completed over ten thousand words on a new book, *A Farewell to Arms*. Ernest's parents, selfishly concerned about their Florida real estate investment, traveled first to St. Petersburg then on to visit their son in Key West. They were curious about the island and its attraction for their son and new daughter-in-law. As Ernest and Pauline's apartment was small, the elder Hemingways stayed at the Overseas Hotel. After his parents' visit, Ernest's primary concern was finding a location for Pauline to have the baby by the end of June.[24]

Tactical, witty and gregarious, Ernest Hemingway began forming friendships through popular island activities. For example, on one of his afternoon fishing trips he met George Brooks, a charismatic Key West attorney, purely by chance.[25] Striking up a conversation about sharing expenses for fishing excursions, Brooks recommended Hemingway stop by the Thompson Hardware Store and introduce himself to Charles Thompson.

And Hemingway took the suggestion. Thompson's family was well known and well off (Charles's older brother Carl [Karl] was the sheriff in Key West). Charles, an avid hunter and fisherman, ran the local hardware store, and when he wasn't behind the counter making a sale, he was likely aboard his eighteen-foot motorboat. As the conversation progressed, it became clear that both participants had a lot in common. Accepting a dinner invitation from Charles and Lorine Thompson, Ernest and Pauline couldn't have been in finer company. It was clear that the basis for a good friendship was there.

After a few local excursions, Hemingway pressed Thompson to join him on a weekend trip to the Marquesas Keys, about thirty miles west of Key West, or halfway to the Dry Tortugas. At first, Thompson balked at the idea of such a trip; moreover, in order to do so, he needed someone to cover for him at the hardware store or, if not, make the decision to close it. Equally as pressing was the exigency for someone capable of navigating the dangerous Rebecca Shoals near the Tortugas. Enter the experienced Captain Eddie "Bra(w)" Saunders, a Bahamian who had migrated to Key West years earlier and knew the shallow water and sandbars like the back of his hand. Thankfully, for everyone involved, the pieces fell into place.

It was this trip that sold Ernest Hemingway on Key West. His dream of fishing, for sailfish and marlin, in the deep blue waters of the Gulf Stream had finally been realized. Part of the billfish family, marlin and sailfish are predatory species. They are quick—capable of taking a fishing line deep at an accelerated pace—and intense fighters. Proving as exhilarating as Hemingway had imagined, the trip was an unforgettable memory. He could recall every moment of landing his first large sailfish; moreover, it was as though it took place in slow motion. His personal guided tour of the complex waters of the Marquesas Keys was safe and unforgettable, all thanks to Charles and Bra.[26]

Aggressively targeting the Dry Tortugas for their next excursion, Hemingway and Thompson began making plans. The Tortugas outing was an opportunity, Ernest believed, to integrate his friends from the past with his new island acquaintances.[27] Invitations were quickly sent out to artists Henry "Mike" Strater and Waldo "Don Pico" Peirce, lifelong friend Bill "Old Bill" Smith and writer John Dos Passos. Once his guests began arriving, they checked into the Overseas Hotel over on Fleming Street. Ernest couldn't wait to introduce them to his Key West accomplices: newspaperman Earl "Jewfish" Adams, fisherman Hamilton "Sacka Ham" Adams, charter boat captain Jakie Key, speakeasy and charter boat owner Joe "Josie" Russell (Sloppy Joe's owner), Captain Eddie "Bra" Saunders and his half brother Burge (Berge) Saunders, machine shop owner J.B. "Sully" Sullivan and Charles Thompson. Naturally, Hemingway wanted to see his old friends, but they were also there to support the literary claims he had been making. As the May days turned to weeks, a routine developed as everyone got to know one another. It wasn't long before the group had their favorite places to drink and dine, along with preferred diversions that ranged from bookstore safaris to swimming hole exhibitions.

During the afternoons, the group bottom fished in the channels for permit, tarpon and snapper while planning the evening's jaunts. Returning to the marina to drop off their catch, part of the group might head home, while the others would hit the Navy Yard for a quick swim. Everyone would meet out for cocktails at a place like Pena's Garden of Roses (beer garden), before selecting their dinner location. Be it the Delmonico Restaurant or Ramon's Restaurant, a hearty meal would be followed by a nightcap at a "speaks" (speakeasy) of choice. Ernest would bow out gracefully before midnight, handing control of the mob over to his adjutant of choice. Dividing, or should we say balancing, his time between writing and fishing was never easy. But it was necessary.[28]

Ernest Hemingway's life was entering revitalization phase. He had a new wife (pregnant with the couple's first child), a new book underway (*A Farewell to Arms*) and a new set of friends in a location that held nothing but promise. The trick, as he would later realize, was balancing the potential in pleasure against that of publication—there was more than one book here, and he knew it.

THE DRY TORTUGAS

Hemingway's Mob, in two boats, set out for the Dry Tortugas on Friday evening the third week of May. Captain "Bra" Saunders hosted Archie, Dos, Ernest, Mike Strater and Waldo in his boat. Charles, who gave up a weekend at the store, was aboard his craft along with "Burge" Saunders. By sundown, the Mob was at the Marquesas catching dinner. At anchor in the shallows, the rum flowed freely before it was time to bed down.

Up at dawn, it was a quick breakfast before heading out in search of tarpon. It didn't take long to find a school. Leave it to Waldo Peirce, or "Don Pico," to spend two hours landing a 138½-pound giant tarpon.[29] Early Sunday, the Marquesas leg of the trip drew to a conclusion, as Charles headed back to Key West, while the others were off to the Dry Tortugas. At

Aerial view of Fort Jefferson, which was part of Fort Jefferson National Monument from 1935 to 1992. Since then, it has been part of Dry Tortugas National Park. *Library of Congress, HABS FLA, 44-1.*

dusk, the group finally reached and tied up at the Fort Jefferson docks. From this point forward, it was all about fighting tarpon, landing snapper and yellowfish and collecting conch and crawfish.

Treated to Captain Bra's mesmerizing tale of being the first boat to reach the doomed Spanish ocean liner *Valbanera* captivated everyone during their final evening at the Fort. The liner was blown off course by the 1919 hurricane and ran aground near the Rebecca Lighthouse. Ernest never forgot Bra's tale of looking through a porthole and seeing a dead woman laden with jewels floating inside; consequently, the account surfaces in Ernest's short story "After the Storm."

The ten-hour ride back to Key West was time to review the trip's highlights. Consciously or not, Ernest was storing every detail of the trip for future use—the author lived his source material. For example, years later, the aging and ailing hands of Captain Bra would be transformed into those of Santiago in the Hemingway classic *The Old Man and the Sea.*[30] As members of the Mob returned home and settled into their daily routines, Hemingway faced reality: His seven weeks in Key West were coming to an end.[31]

Off the Island

As for the highlights off the island: Patrick Miller Hemingway was born via caesarean section on June 28, 1928, in Kansas City, Missouri. And he weighed an impressive nine and a half pounds. Ernest met a local furniture maker in Piggott named T. Otto "Toby" Bruce. While Hemingway was impressed by the eighteen-year-old, they would not meet again until the fall of 1935; Ernest headed off to Wyoming at the end of July to fish and finish his book. Returning to Piggott, Ernest traveled to Chicago and Toronto in October.[32]

ERNEST, PAULINE AND PATRICK arrived back in Key West in November. Thanks to Lorine Thompson, the Hemingway clan rented a wood-frame house at 1100 South Street. In addition to Ernest and Pauline living at the residence, Patrick was assisted by a nurse (Olive), while Ernest's sister Madelaine, aka "Sunny," was there to type Ernest's manuscript. Not long after their arrival, Ernest headed to New York to pick up Bumby, who had sailed from France, and to do a bit of Christmas shopping. On December 8, 1928, while traveling by train with his son back to Florida, Ernest Hemingway was informed by telegram of the death of his father. With few options, Ernest wired Mike Strater and F. Scott Fitzgerald for money, entrusted his son to the care of a porter and hurried west to Chicago.[33]

Arriving in Oak Park, Ernest learned of the details: Depressed, suffering from diabetes and unsure of his future, Dr. Clarence Edmonds "Ed" Hemingway shot himself with his father's Smith and Wesson .32 revolver. The one parent Ernest *really* cared about was now gone. After tending to affairs, Ernest headed back to Key West.

1929

Family life was hectic but tolerable considering the circumstances. Once Ernest arrived, he finished his revision of *A Farewell to Arms*. Max "Deadpan" Perkins from Scribner's traveled to Key West to collect the typescript. Once the editor accepted the manuscript, it was all about fishing and enjoying the family.

The Mob, consisting of Dos, Ernest, Mike Strater, Waldo and Max Perkins, hired Captain Bra's charter boat in the spring for a trip to the Dry Tortugas. Fishing in and around Fort Jefferson, the group slept on Saunders's boat or right on the docks. One night, a small Cuban motorboat pulled up to the pier. Ever hospitable, Ernest invited them over for a rum swap, which they did while sharing Gulf Stream yarns. The colorful captain of the vessel was Carlos Gutierrez of Havana, Cuba, who would later become a fishing advisor and mate aboard Hemingway's boat.

It was about this time, while living at South Street, that Ernest began attracting enough attention to be considered a local celebrity. Much of this was courtesy of Scribner's, which was driving publicity for *A Farewell to Arms*. While most of the out-of-town media was annoying, Hemingway did make friends with Earl Adams, who had a bureau job with the *Miami Herald*. The two met by chance while fishing on the Niles Key Bridge. In April, it was time to pack and prepare for the crossing to Havana, then on to France to return Jack to his mother. Before leaving, Ernest instructed the Thompsons to find him an even bigger home. The Hemingway clan left Havana on April 5, 1929, and arrived in Boulogne aboard the *Yorck* on April 21. Ernest would not return to Key West for ten months.

Off the Island

As for the highlights off the island: While in Paris, Ernest was busy correcting galleys for *A Farewell to Arms*.[34] However, he did have time to do some sparring with Morley Callaghan. The Hemingways left for Pamplona, Spain, on July 2 and stayed at the Hotel Quintana. Ernest enjoyed a pleasant visit with artist Joan Miro, whom he had met in Paris.[35] While in Spain, Ernest traveled the bullfighting circuit—he also learned of the marriage of John Dos Passos to Katharine "Kate" Foster Smith while there. Back in Paris by the first week of October, the family used the city as a hub for their European travels until January 1930.

1930

The Hemingways (Ernest, Pauline, Patrick and Sunny), arrived in New York on January 23, 1930, and were anxious to return to Key West. Arriving on the island the second week of February, they took up residence at a rented apartment on Pearl Street—a stone's throw from Route One and Garrison Bight. (This section of Pearl Street, near Jose Marti Drive, no longer exists.) Nationally recognized for the success of *A Farewell to Arms*, Ernest

Hemingway treated himself to another run to the Dry Tortugas. Renting a cabin cruiser, Ernest, along with Mob members Burge Saunders, Mike Strater, Max Perkins and John Herrmann, headed out in mid-March for their weeklong journey. As fate might have it, an intense tropical storm forced them to remain out for seventeen days. Fortunately, the Mob was able to stretch their food and water supply while docked at Fort Jefferson.[36]

Once back home, Hemingway turned his attention to two projects: an African safari and a nonfiction book about bullfighting.[37] As work began on the latter, the oppressive June heat signaled Ernest that it was time to pack up Pauline, Patrick and Patrick's nurse and send them back to Piggott, while he headed to New York to pick up Bumby. Ernest and Bumby would then drive to Arkansas. It was clear by this point that Key West was becoming home, so why not find a house of their own? Ernest spent time looking for an alternative with Charles Thompson, as did Pauline with Lorine. A neglected two-story house at 907 Whitehead Street—in exigency of repair and landscaping, yet in a good location—would soon become their choice.

OFF THE ISLAND

Having his fill of Piggott by mid-July, Ernest, Pauline and Bumby (Patrick would stay with family) headed west to Wyoming and Montana.[38] This would give Ernest an opportunity to write in the cool morning air while hunting (in preparation for his African safari) and fishing in the afternoon sun. As the month of October ended, Ernest was close to completing a quality draft of *Death in the Afternoon*. On November 1, after transporting Dos Passos to a train station in Billings, Montana, Hemingway was involved in an automobile accident. A compound spiral fracture to his right arm required weeks of hospitalization at St. Vincent's Hospital in Billings, Montana.[39] It was during this time, in a dictated letter to Charles Thompson, that Ernest for the first time referred to himself as "poor ole Papa." And in a letter to Archibald MacLeish, he closed by signing "Pappy." Although the author often signed his letters in full, or "Ernest," or "Hem," or "Ernesto," his moniker "Papa" would gradually become his favorite. He was released from the hospital before Christmas, and the Hemingway clan headed to Piggott, then on to Key West.[40]

1931

The Hemingways' third residence was a rented two-story wood-frame house on the corner of Whitehead and United Streets (a block from what would be billed as the "southernmost point in the U.S.A."). For this season of the Mob, Ernest was joined by John Herrmann and his wife, Josephine Herbst; Lawrence and Olive Nordquist; Max Perkins; "Josie" Russell; Captain Bra and Burge Saunders; Sully Sullivan; Charles and Lorine Thompson; and Chub Weaver.[41]

It was one of the more memorable excursions: Ernest rented Albert Pinder's charter boat so that he, along with John Herrmann, Max Perkins, Burge Saunders and Chub Weaver, could head to the Dry Tortugas.[42] Juicy, with a sweet onion flavor, Bermuda onions were a staple of Ernest Hemingway's diet. White or yellow, these flat-topped onions were typically found in salads and soups or on sandwiches. But on the water, Hemingway

Ernest Hemingway and friends aboard the *Anita* with a marlin in Key West, Florida. *Left to right*: Ernest Hemingway, Carlos Gutierrez, Joe "Sloppy Joe"/"Josie" Russell (owner of the *Anita*) and Joe Lowe, circa 1933. *Ernest Hemingway Collection. John F. Kennedy Presidential Library and Museum, Boston.*

ate them like apples. Running out of onions, he boarded a nearby fishing smack to purchase some. It was on this boat—the author had never seen a cleaner or more organized watercraft—that Ernest met Canary Islander Gregorio Fuentes, who would be immortalized in *The Old Man and the Sea*. But it was also during this trip that a ferocious storm struck the Tortugas and the group ran low on supplies. Since Max Perkins had to leave early, he returned on the boat that was sent back to replenish the Mob's provisions. Unfortunately, engine trouble delayed Pinder's boat during the return voyage. The group was forced to make do with what they had. Later, aboard Joe Russell's charter boat *Anita*, a thirty-two-foot cabin cruiser, Ernest and Charles made a few crossings over to Havana.[43]

By 1931, Key West resembled Havana, Cuba. Gambling, prostitution and rooster fights were as common as fishing boats. Nevertheless, the Hemingway clan officially called it home on April 29, 1931, when they bought 907 Whitehead Street, which was a combination of about two hundred feet on Whitehead Street and two hundred feet on Olivia Street. But rather than immediately refurbishing their large Spanish Colonial estate, Ernest decided to leave for Spain so that he could finish *Death in the Afternoon*. As for the rest of the family, they were off to Paris.

Off the Island

From May until September 1931, Ernest followed the bullfighting circuit in Spain. In Kansas City, on November 12, 1931, Ernest and Pauline welcomed their second child, Gregory Hancock Hemingway. Early in December, it was back to Piggott to introduce the new addition to his relatives. Returning to Key West, the Hemingway clan was in their new home by mid-December. It was the first home Ernest Hemingway had owned in ten years of married life, and like a blank piece of paper, the property held potential. Over the next eight years, the mythos of Ernest Miller Hemingway would grow exponentially. This was *his* time, and he knew it.

1932

While it felt good to be back in Key West, the condition of the home during the renovation presented a challenge. Pauline, often with a child in each hand, was doing her best to keep order in the house. Still weak from her caesarean childbirth, she was also supervising much of the challenging restoration—this as plaster was falling from the ceiling over her son's crib.

Meantime, Ernest retired to a two-story outbuilding at the back of the house. Once a carriage house, there was a servant's quarters on the second floor he hoped to convert to a writing studio. Though it was little more than a storage area at the time, Ernest was able to create a small workspace, thanks to a cigar makers' chair and a small round table. Navigating between the boxes that littered the room reminded him of how Bra Saunders twisted and turned his watercraft through the Marquesas.

While Ernest dedicated his time to *Death in the Afternoon*, Pauline went about hiring domestic workers, including a cook, gardener, washwoman and butler. Overseeing the staff was Ada Stern, who hailed from Syracuse, New York. She ran a tight ship, and that was precisely what was needed.

Taking a brief break from his writing in February and early March, Ernest, along with Charles Thompson and Captain "Bra" Saunders, headed to the Tortugas.[44] In April, he and Joe Russell traveled to Cuba aboard the *Anita* for what turned out to be a two-month visit.[45] Ernest checked into the five-story Hotel Ambos Mundos on Obispo Street in Havana. From his fifth-floor room (No. 511), he read his galley proofs of *Death in the Afternoon*, taking short breaks to admire the view of the harbor and the cathedral—Pauline even visited him twice.[46] When Pauline didn't take her seat aboard the *Anita*, it was willingly filled by acquaintance Jane Mason, who lived west of Havana. Both Ernest and Josie returned again in June. That month, Pauline and family (along with Ada Stern) entrained to Piggott. Ernest and his youngest sister, Carol, followed in the Ford and were in Piggott by the end of the first week of July.

Off the Island

After a short visit in Piggott, Ernest and Pauline drove to the Nordquist Ranch (Wyoming) near Yellowstone Park. Charles Thompson visited in September, as he and Ernest were refining their skills for a proposed African safari the following year. Missing the boys, Pauline returned to Piggott on September 22. In early October, Scribner's published *Death in the Afternoon* to mixed reviews.

During the third week of October, Charles Thompson and Ernest left Wyoming and headed to Key West. Pauline was there, as was Bumby; however, the former left for Piggott on word the other two boys were sick there.[47] Later, Ernest drove to Piggott for the movie premiere of *A Farewell to Arms*.[48]

1933

By mid-January, Ernest and Pauline, along with all three boys and Ada Stern, were back in Key West. On February 9, Ernest made the front page of the *Key West Citizen*, as the movie version of his famous novel *A Farewell To Arms* would soon be shown (beginning on February 11) at the Strand Theater on Duval Street. While Ernest was excited at the announcement, he wasn't happy to see his home address in the article.

With Prohibition drawing to a close, Hemingway wanted to catch Josie Russell for some serious marlin fishing before his bar turned "legit," as they say. As the author was forming the "Harry Morgan Stories," the companionship made sense. Russell would become the fictional charter boat captain "Harry Morgan," as well as a fictional bartender named "Freddy"—the Morgan stories were published by Scribner's as *To Have and Have Not*. Aboard the *Anita*, the pair headed to Cuba on April 12 and stayed for weeks. Hemingway also secured the services of Carlos Gutierrez—the Cuban fishing captain and guide he met back in 1929. On July 10, Hemingway once again was featured on the front page of the local newspaper. This time it was for landing a 468-pound marlin off Morro Castle in Cuba. After over an hour of play, the author finally brought his trophy aboard the *Anita* with the assistance of Captain Russell. They returned to Key West during the third week of July. Helping to finance the trip was a series of articles Hemingway agreed to submit to Arnold Gingrich's new men's magazine called *Esquire*.[49] He also hoped to use the revenue generated by the periodical for a down payment on a boat. On August 4, Ernest and Pauline and their children, along with Charles and Lorine Thompson, sailed for Havana. Ernest and Charles planned to enjoy a few days of marlin fishing before the Thompsons returned to Key West and the Hemingway clan proceeded to Europe (August 7)—Pauline's sister Jinny accompanied them to Paris.

Off the Island

Ernest and Pauline Hemingway would not set foot in Key West for nine months. In typical Hemingway fashion, the logistics involved with Ernest's travel aspirations were challenging. Pauline and her sister remained in Paris—they were waiting for the arrival of Charles Thompson in November—while Ernest covered the bullfighting circuit in Spain. The group sailed to Africa on November 22. Although Key West may have been home, Ernest Hemingway was not spending much of his time there. But that would soon change.[50]

1934

Having concluded their global travels, Ernest and Pauline arrived in New York in April.[51] While his party headed home to Key West, Ernest stayed behind to order his thirty-eight-foot custom boat at the Wheeler Shipyard (City Island, New York).[52] After a seven-month absence, the author boarded a train for home. Hemingway was astonished when he stepped from his Pullman—the Havana Special from New York arrived in Key West on April 11—and was greeted by a jazz band along with his friends and family. As Papa was considered a celebrity, his arrival was front-page news in the *Key West Citizen*. While notoriety was a byproduct of being a bestselling author, Hemingway preferred a favorable review or a sizable royalty check over a reception.[53]

Ernest tried to remain patient while his custom watercraft was built, but it wasn't easy. Finally, he received word that his fishing boat, which the author would call *Pilar*, had arrived in Miami by rail. Next stop Key West, but that meant sailing the craft south. After he talked Captain Bra Saunders into accompanying him by train to Miami on May 9, the pair prepared themselves for the *Pilar*'s initial voyage. Meantime, the remaining members of the Mob planned to meet their friends at the submarine pen, where Hemingway had received permission to berth free of charge. Conveniently located, *Pilar* was moored to a dock only a few blocks from 907 Whitehead Street.

Having begun what would be *The Green Hills of Africa*, Hemingway once again balanced his time between writing and fishing. Between his work and his new toy, the author couldn't have been happier. Accompanied by available Mob members, along with new shipmates Arnold Samuelson, Les (Hemingway), Al (Dudek) and Carlos Gutierrez, Hemingway gradually tested *Pilar*'s capabilities against those of the captain and his hands.[54]

With Prohibition behind him, Joe Russell was one busy saloon owner. Having vacated his Front Street speakeasy in 1933, Sloppy Joe's was now serving customers at 428 Greene Street. Hemingway would have loved to have Russell aboard the *Pilar*, but the saloon owner had to decline. With the majority of Key West unemployed, and both the County of Monroe and the City of Key West unable to pay their employees, washing away your troubles at Sloppy Joe's was far from an answer, but it was an alternative. And the Great Depression, having claimed the cigar industry, crippled the fishing industry and clobbered local government, wasn't over. The Federal Emergency Relief Administration (FERA), in an attempt to solve the problem, initiated a program for the county and city to rehabilitate the island.

Desperate to get *Pilar* out on the blue water for its first big cruise, Hemingway and crew joined hands with the Academy of Natural Sciences (located in Philadelphia) on a marlin fishing study off the coast of Cuba.[55] The party left Key West on July 19 for what would amount to a six-week fishing expedition. Upon returning to Key West in September via a P.&O. steamship, Hemingway dove back into the *Green Hills of Africa*—the author finished a first draft on November 16. Needing a good cleaning, not to mention a tune-up, *Pilar* remained docked in Havana. In December, the Hemingway clan made the 1,600-mile trek to Piggott to celebrate Christmas.[56]

1935

Back in Key West in January, Ernest, recovering from a bout of dysentery, was preparing himself mentally and physically for a fishing expedition to the island of Bimini, fifty miles off the coast of Miami. Granted there were a number of afternoon sessions at Sloppy Joe's—the author was celebrating the serialization rights of *The Green Hills of Africa* to *Scribner's Magazine*—but the book still needed proofing.[57] Hemingway, along with his Mob members—John Dos Passos, Kate Dos Passos, Henry "Mike" Strater, Charles Thompson (who came later), Albert "Bread" Pinter and Hamilton "Sacka Ham" Adams—headed to Bimini on April 7, 1935. With the departure of Arnold "Maestro" Samuelson, Pinter was being groomed for helmsman of *Pilar*. This was the excursion that would witness Hemingway shooting himself in both legs while trying to kill a boarded shark (more on this later). Returning to Key West, the same group—minus Mike Strater, who was replaced by Charles Thompson—tried again when their captain healed.

Ernest did take a break in June—he briefly returned to Key West to see the kids. Hitchhiking south, "Toby" Bruce joined the Hemingway family in June and, under Ernest's instruction, began building a wall around the Whitehead Street residence—thankfully, he finished before hurricane season. Toby Bruce then headed back to Piggott, Arkansas. The author had become a tourist attraction, and the wall was an attempt to preserve his privacy.

Hemingway and the Mob formally departed Bimini in August, and Ernest went right to work correcting the proofs for *The Green Hills of Africa*. As though on cue, the worst hurricane to ever hit the Keys struck.[58] Learning of the storm's approach, Hemingway was concerned about the *Pilar*. Since the harbor men couldn't lift it out of the water—they were busy removing their own watercraft—Ernest moved it to the safest corner of the submarine base. The hurricane, which landed at the upper keys (Upper and Lower Matecumbe), destroyed everything in its path, including over 175 miles of track from the Key West Extension. Initial death estimates were as high as one thousand—later, over four hundred fatalities were confirmed.

Ernest left Key West in September and headed to New York City for a sporting event—the author paid for the trip by covering the Joe Louis versus Max Baer heavyweight fight for *Esquire*. The Yankee Stadium battle was well worth the time, as Max Baer was floored for the first time in his career in round three and knocked out in round four. Working as a second in Baer's corner was Jack Dempsey. Naturally, Hemingway, who never cared for Dempsey after the heavyweight refused to spar with him, was happy to witness the result. The author returned to New York City again the following month to experience firsthand the mixed reviews for *The Green Hills of Africa*.[59]

1936

From January until April, Ernest filled his time conducting fishing excursions with the Mob and assorted guests such as actress Nancy Carroll and Jane Mason—the former visitor more of a one-off guest, while the latter a far more familiar countenance.[60] Even Captain Hemingway agreed that it never hurt to have a pretty face aboard. On April 26, Ernest and Joe Russell, along with Jane Mason, headed off to Cuba and stayed until the end of May.[61] Returning to Key West, he soon set off for Miami with Patrick and an ailing Carlos Gutierrez aboard *Pilar*.

After an engine replacement for the craft, the group headed to Bimini, Ernest's newfound treasure.[62] Prior to his thirty-sixth birthday, he headed back to Key West. Having spoken to Arnold Gingrich in June—the pair discussed the third Harry Morgan short story, along with the possibility of combining all of stories into a novel, or what would be *To Have and Have Not*—he felt good about the direction of his work. Productive during the month of July, Hemingway also managed to sell two crafted short stories:

Esquire purchased "The Snows of Kilimanjaro" (published August 1936), and *Cosmopolitan* bought "The Short Happy Life of Francis Macomber" (published September 1936).[63] As the hot August nights began to take hold, the Hemingway family (Ernest, Pauline, Patrick and Gregory) headed to the Nordquist L-Bar-T Ranch in Wyoming.

Ernest returned to Key West via Piggott in October; only this time, it was Toby Bruce behind the wheel and not the author—Ernest had hired him as a driver. Upon their arrival, Ernest, realizing the need for a much larger vehicle, sent Toby to purchase a new Buick Special Convertible from the Mulberg Chevrolet Company—the author had been eyeing the car for some time. Ernest was delighted by the purchase. From this point forward, Toby Bruce became the author's salaried assistant.

The bulk of the fall was spent working on the Harry Morgan stories, aka *To Have and Have Not*. Ernest adhered to a regimented schedule. Yes, there were plenty of quarter-priced scotch and sodas at Sloppy Joe's but never before 2:00 p.m.

Martha Gellhorn

In December 1936, Martha Ellis Gellhorn, over a decade younger than Ernest Hemingway, appeared in Key West. As an American journalist who had published both a novel, *What Mad Pursuit*, and collection of short stories, *The Trouble I've Seen*, her overflowing ambition was as clear as her bright blond hair and welcoming smile. She had come to the island on vacation with her mother and brother, but there was far more behind the journey. Though the details of the story have changed a bit over the years, Martha Gellhorn met Ernest Hemingway inside Sloppy Joe's (Captain Tony's Saloon)—Marty, as she was called, was very familiar with the author's work. Their friendship grew quickly, and when Marty's mother and brother departed the island, she remained behind. Hemingway was enthralled by Gellhorn's passion for adventure—it was as though he was looking in the mirror. Whereas Ernest's involvement with Marty appeared to elude Pauline, it did not escape the disapproving eyes of Charles and Lorine Thompson.

During this period, Hemingway, along with several other literary figures, including John Dos Passos, Archibald MacLeish and Dorothy Parker, backed an anti-fascist film project called *The Spanish Earth*. Made during the Spanish Civil War, the film was directed by Joris Ivens.[64]

Ernest Hemingway's passport during a portion of his stay in Key West. *John F. Kennedy Presidential Library and Museum, Boston.*

1937

Martha Gellhorn left Key West by car in late January and drove to Miami. She was on her way back to her home in St. Louis. Clandestinely, Ernest met Marty in Miami before each went their separate way.[65] Ernest went to New York to arrange covering the Spanish Civil War with the North American Newspaper Alliance (NANA). He would sail to France aboard *Paris* on February 27.[66] Hemingway flew with Joris Ivens from France into Spain on March 16, 1937, to complete filming *The Spanish Earth*. Martha Gellhorn was in Spain covering the war for *Collier's* magazine. Hemingway returned to New York aboard *Normandie* on May 18 and then flew home to Key West. It was upon his return that the moniker "Papa" was affixed to the author. As he was a novelist of international fame, the nickname seemed to fit.

In late May, Ernest and family boarded the *Pilar* bound for Bimini (Bahamas).[67] The goal of the trip was to enjoy some good fishing, finish his novel and repair any damage to his relationship with Pauline. The visit would face two interruptions: a speech in June at the Second American Writers' Congress in New York and a visit to the White House. President Franklin D. Roosevelt, along with First Lady Eleanor Roosevelt, invited Hemingway

Pauline Pfeiffer, Ernest Hemingway, Jack "Bumby" Hemingway, Patrick "Mouse" Hemingway and Gregory "Gigi" Hemingway with four marlins on the dock in Bimini, Bahamas. *Ernest Hemingway Collection. John F. Kennedy Presidential Library and Museum, Boston.*

and Joris Ivens to the White House for an advance screening of the film *The Spanish Earth* on July 8, 1937—this courtesy of Martha Gellhorn. While moved by the film, the Roosevelts believed it needed more propaganda. By the way: Hemingway was charmed by Eleanor Roosevelt but not so impressed with her husband.

Ernest hoped to return to Spain by August and did precisely that.[68] He flew to New York to connect with a liner bound for the Iberian Peninsula while the rest of the family left Key West bound for Mexico.

OFF THE ISLAND

Ernest's time with Marty developed into a play called *The Fifth Column* (Ernest playing the role of Philip Rawlings and Marty as Dorothy Bridges).[69] It was as close, according to some critics, to an autobiography as Hemingway would ever get. With hopes of saving her marriage, Pauline left the children in Key West and headed to Paris to meet Ernest. At the conclusion of a heated discussion, Ernest agreed to quit the war and return to Key West with Pauline.[70]

1938

In an attempt to preoccupy Ernest, Pauline installed a large swimming pool in the backyard. It didn't work. Instead, it provoked the author into tossing a penny at her and claiming she may as well have his last cent—the penny was stamped permanently into the pool edge. Ernest was miserable. Frequently drowning his sorrows at Sloppy Joe's—the previous summer the bar had moved from its Greene Street location over to Duval Street—he was determined to return to Spain, which he did at the end of March.[71] The exhilaration of covering the war lasted two months. That was when the guilt set in, and Ernest decided to return to Key West.[72] Nearly a decade since he first set foot in the tropical paradise, it appeared that his days on the island were drawing to a close. Upon his arrival, he received a lukewarm welcome from his friends and family. However, revising his play and meeting story deadlines persuaded him to stay.[73] Key West was undergoing a change, and Ernest could sense it on many levels. One of shifts was the tourists who waited across the street from his Whitehead Street home in anticipation of catching a photograph or even a sidewalk audience with the author.[74]

No stranger to symbolism, Ernest Hemingway headed to New York City in June for the rematch between Joe Louis and Max Schmeling. The world had changed since Schmeling defeated Louis in 1936. Hitler's anti-Semitic ideologies, along with his Third Reich propaganda machine, had the entire world nervous. Schmeling, who once represented only himself, had become a symbol of Nazi Germany. Although Schmeling was neither a member of the Nazi Party nor advocated their claims of racial superiority, he had little choice but to become a pawn in the entire affair. It took Joe Louis a mere two minutes and four seconds to settle the score.

Returning home, Ernest managed to persuade Joe Russell and his son to make another run with him to Cuba. With the *Pilar* under repair, the trio boarded Russell's *Anita* and headed out—they picked up a crew in Havana and went in search of marlin. Between domestic life and the summer heat, the island was wearing thin on the author. Rather than returning to Spain, he agreed to take the family out to Wyoming for a stopover at the Nordquist Ranch. The dedication found in *The Fifth Column and the First Forty-Nine Stories* essentially sealed his domestic fate: "To Marty and Herbert (a journalist he had met in Spain) with Love." During the final days of August, Ernest headed back to Spain—he stayed there with Marty until November.[75] Ernest briefly rejoined Pauline and the boys in New York at her apartment on East 50th Street before returning to Key West on December 5.[76]

1939

From his room at the Ambos Mundos Hotel in Havana, Hemingway stared out at the city, reflecting on his life in Key West. He was working on a new novel about the Spanish Civil War that he would call *For Whom the Bell Tolls*. In March, he flew back over to Key West to visit with his son Jack, who was on holiday. Calling on all three boys was enjoyable, as was working in his old studio, but it felt different—it was like trying on a coat that no longer fit.

On April 10, Ernest headed back to Cuba, where he would be joined by Marty a week later. The pair rented an old estate on the outskirts of Havana called "La Viga" (The Watchtower). Set amid the rolling hills on the outskirts of San Francisco de Paula, the estate was a mere twenty-minute drive to Havana. There, Hemingway continued work on *For Whom the Bell Tolls*.

In late August, Ernest and Marty headed back to Key West—Pauline was in Europe. Later, Ernest drove Marty to St. Louis before heading out to Wyoming to work. Ironically, Ernest visited with his first wife, Hadley, who happened to be in the state. When Pauline arrived, she once again hoped for a reconciliation. It failed. With divorce clearly on the horizon, Ernest headed to Sun Valley, a resort town in south-central Idaho.[77]

On December 10, Ernest and Toby Bruce drove to Key West. They arrived on December 16 to an empty home on Whitehead Street—Ernest had hoped Pauline and the boys would be there after pleading with her over the phone to remain through the holidays.[78] While at the house, Hemingway and Bruce began packing up his personal effects to be placed in storage. It was reported that Ernest, along with his son Patrick and Toby Bruce, departed Key West for Havana on December 24.

1940

In a proceeding that lasted one hour, Ernest Hemingway was divorced from his second wife, Pauline Pfeiffer Hemingway, on November 4, 1940. The marriage had lasted thirteen years, five months and twenty-five days, excluding the end date. Neither of the principals was in Key West.

Ernest Hemingway married Martha Gellhorn on November 20, 1940, in Cheyenne, Wyoming. The ceremony was performed by the justice of the peace of that city. Hemingway's latest novel, *For Whom The Bell Tolls*, was dedicated to his new bride.

In December, Hemingway was back in Key West visiting his sons Patrick and Gregory while his ex-wife was in Arkansas.[79] Hemingway continued removing whatever items he could from the home on Whitehead Street and instructed Toby Bruce to pack up the rest. Much of it was stored in the back room of Sloppy Joe's and retrieved only after the author's death on the morning of July 2, 1961.[80]

2

HEMINGWAY'S MOB, ASSOCIATES AND ASSORTED GUESTS

B y the time Ernest Hemingway arrived in Key West, he had dedicated himself to fiction writing. For example, *The Sun Also Rises* (1926), or the author's thesis of the "Lost Generation," describes a group of expatriate Americans and Englishmen, all of whom suffered physically and emotionally during the war. *A Farewell to Arms* (1929) tells the story of a tragically terminated love affair between an American soldier and an English nurse, silhouetted against the bleakness of war and a deteriorating world order. However, nonfiction was not off limits, particularly if it involved an interesting opportunity. Take bullfighting in Spain for example: *Death in the Afternoon* was proof that a dangerous ritual transcended sport.[81] There was an art to prose writing in both forms, and the author was committed to it.

The English poet John Keats once quipped, "Nothing ever becomes real 'til it is experienced." Hemingway agreed and did not allow his fiction to drift too far from reality. Since experience was enhanced by opportunity, he understood that a group of people supplemented both. A gathering of people, or mob if you will, also had more influence or power than one person. Assembling his supporting cast would prove equally as important to Ernest Hemingway in the United States as it was in Europe. Key West, like Paris or Milan, was a new environment and his island friends a fascinating contrast to the Parisian artists of the left bank.[82]

Hemingway's Mob was an entourage consisting of those he could learn from, like charter boat captains or fishermen; those who shared his past experiences, like ambulance drivers and writers; those who shared his

Hemingway's Mob provided advice, confidence, contacts, encouragement, feedback and support. A portrait of the "Old Master." *State Archives of Florida, Florida Memory.*

creativity, like painters and poets; those for whom he could write or who could write about him, like newspapermen and magazine editors; those who were connected, like entrepreneurs and island family members; and even those who were simply there to guarantee the current experience, like mechanics or service technicians. The only thing missing was a heroine or love interest—thankfully, there was always room on the boat. Everyone—and they all knew it—became a target for a future character in one of the author's bestsellers. Immortality, even from a fictional work, is an improvement over no eternal life at all.[83] Writing was a proficiency of perspective, and the author understood the elucidation.

Hemingway's Mob provided advice, confidence, contacts, encouragement, feedback and support. Some acted as mentors for skills Hemingway sought, be it fixing an engine or guiding a watercraft through the dangerous shoals surrounding Key West. Others became sounding boards for new ideas. As an entourage, there was a certain level of accountability assigned to each member—it wasn't always obvious, but it was there—and that made the goal of the group, such as an extended trip to the Dry Tortugas, easier. But the advantage Hemingway treasured most from an entourage was its privacy. As a man who hated public criticism, his entourage was a security blanket. Writing was a veil for his vulnerability, and the author used it as such.

The demarcation between Ernest Hemingway's writing and the Key West lifestyle was indistinct, but it fit the novelist like a glove.

A CAST OF CHARACTERS

They were a band of brothers, Hemingway's Mob. From the crooked cap and smile of "Josie Grunts," to the roaring laughter of "Don Pico," there was never a dull moment. Availability determined a Mob member's attendance on an excursion. However, there were times when a particular skill set was needed, like that of Captain "Bra" Saunders, who assisted Hemingway guiding the *Pilar* during its initial voyage to Key West. If "Old

Hem" fancied your company, you were given a moniker—masculinity had its boundaries of affection. The act was unpretentious and created "a level playing field" aboard his watercraft. As relationships are never perfect, Hemingway did have a falling out with a Mob member or two, a good example being Archibald MacLeish. But as one member fell out, another was quickly added.

Without further ado, allow me to present "Hemingway's Mob." (Those who are not regular Hemingway Mob members are indicated by an asterisk.) Hemingway's monikers appear between a Mob member's name and occupation.

Earl R. Adams—"Jewfish," Newspaperman

The son of Thomas and Blanche Adams, Earl Richard Adams (December 29, 1902–September 20, 1993) was a delightful addition to the Hemingway Mob. Standing five feet nine inches and weighing about 135 pounds, his lighter complexion contrasted with the tattoo on his right arm. Adams had striking blue eyes and black hair. As a successful newspaperman, he was employed by the *Key West Citizen*, the *Key West Morning Journal* and the *Miami Herald*. His regular column "Do You Know," which appeared in the *Key West Citizen*, was extraordinarily popular. Later, Adams was a court clerk for Monroe County from 1949 until 1973. According to census data, Earl and his wife, Linnie, along with their children, were living at 917 Angela Street in 1940. Adams died at the age of ninety and was buried in the Key West Cemetery.

(Richard) Hamilton Adams—"Sacka Ham," Charter Boat Fisherman

"Sacka Ham" (December 27, 1889–October 30, 1969) was a tall drink of water, as they used to say, with a slender build and eyes as blue as the waters of the gulf. As a successful fishing guide, he was respected for his knowledge. Hemingway loved the way Adams instinctively navigated a boat about the sea.

While his wife, Mary (Roberts) Adams, who was thirteen years younger, handled the two children (Marilyn and Richard) at their rented home on the Oversea Highway, "Ham" worked the water. He loved every minute of it, and it showed. When Adams became involved with the Key West Aquarium, nobody was surprised, but they were certainly grateful.

On his World War I Civilian Draft Registration, Adams listed his address as 412 Grinnell Street in Key West.

(Richard) Hamilton Adams Jr.—"Sacka Ham," Sponge Fisherman

Richard Hamilton Adams Jr. "Sacka Ham" (January 13, 1938–May 10, 2003) became a sponge fisherman after a stint in the U.S. Army (1955–58). Later in life, he listed his residence as 1016 James Street in Key West. Both father and son were buried in the Key West Cemetery.

*George Gray Brooks—"Georgie," Key West Attorney

Born in Key West, George Gray Brooks Jr. (1905–1969) became a prominent local attorney and a politician. Standing five feet seven inches high and weighing only about 125 pounds, he was a handsome and charismatic man who had blond hair and brown eyes. It was a young George Brooks who struck up a conversation one day with the newly arrived Hemingway and recommended that Ernest contact Charles Thompson about chartering a fishing boat. "Georgie" gradually became one of Hemingway's staunchest drinking companions even though he could be as annoying as a seagull over a fresh catch—he had a way of antagonizing folks with practical jokes. In 1940, Brooks resided with his mother at 718 Eaton Street. Brooks would surface as "Bee-lips" in Hemingway's *To Have and Have Not.*

Telly "Otto" Bruce—"Toby," Hemingway's Right-Hand Man

Possessing a skill set enviable to any man, Telly (Tellie) "Otto" or "Toby" Bruce (June 22, 1910–May 9, 1984) met Ernest Hemingway and his second wife, Pauline, in Piggott, Arkansas (1928). Once Ernest and Pauline settled in Key West, they invited Toby along to assist in the remodeling of their Spanish-style mansion on Whitehead Street (1932). From running errands to building a wall around the author's home, Bruce was Ernest's right-hand man. As an expert mechanic, he fine-tuned Hemingway's automobiles and even the *Pilar.* He married Laura Elizabeth "Betty" Moreno in 1942.

Popular, slender and soft-spoken, Bruce operated the Home Appliance Company at 605 Simonton Street for twenty-five years. His wife, Betty Bruce (1918–1994), was a gifted historian at the Monroe County Library. Toby Bruce died in a Miami Hospital at the age of seventy-three. Both he and his wife were buried in Key West Cemetery.

*Nancy Carroll—Actress

Born Ann Veronica Lahiff, Nancy Carroll (November 19, 1903–August 6, 1965) began her career on Broadway. Her prolific movie career (1927–1938) saw notable appearances in *The Devil's Holiday* (1930), *Hot Saturday* (1932) and *The Kiss Before the Mirror* (1933). Although talented, beautiful and popular, she garnered a reputation for being difficult to work with. Fortunate to find herself aboard *Pilar* in February 1936, she would not be a frequent visitor. Quentin Reynolds (1902–1965), nationally known writer for *Collier's*, accompanied Miss Carroll during her Key West visit. As a prolific penman, Reynolds averaged twenty articles a year. He also published twenty-five books, including *The Wounded Don't Cry*, *London Diary*, *Dress Rehearsal* and *Courtroom*.[84]

John Dos Passos—"Dos," Author

John Dos Passos (January 14, 1896–September 28, 1970) served in the American Red Cross Ambulance Service in Italy during World War I. He met Hemingway in June 1918 in Schio (Italy), but years passed before the two renewed and solidified their friendship in Paris (1924). That same year, Dos Passos joined Hemingway at the Fiesta of San Fermín in Pamplona, Spain.

When Katharine Foster "Kate" Smith, from St. Louis, met John Dos Passos, they fell in love. Ernest and Hadley's longtime friend was smitten over the Harvard graduate and impressed by his knowledge of literature, art and architecture. The couple married on August 19, 1929, in Ellsworth, Maine.

At the time of the couple's marriage, John Dos Passos was best known for penning *Manhattan Transfer* (1925) and *Orient Express* (1927). He was working on a book titled *The 42nd Parallel* (1930). French critic Jean-Paul Sartre believed Dos Passos was the best novelist of the 1920s and 1930s.

As a member of the "Lost Generation" of expatriate artists and writers that populated Paris during the 1920s, John Dos Passos was talented and well traveled. And it was on his advice that Ernest Hemingway made

John Dos Passos reading aloud to Katy Dos Passos aboard Joe "Sloppy Joe"/"Josie" Russell's boat, the *Anita*, 1932. *Ernest Hemingway Collection. John F. Kennedy Presidential Library and Museum, Boston.*

his initial visit to Key West. Besides their obvious history and friendship, Dos Passos's role in the Key West Mob was to validate Hemingway's literary claims. Understanding that Hemingway was competitive and critical of others, Dos Passos gradually learned to handle his friend's chest-thumping virility.[85]

Kate Dos Passos—Wife, Family Friend

Born in Barton, Missouri, Katharine Foster Smith (October 26, 1891– September 12, 1947) was a Mary Institute classmate of Hadley Richardson (Hemingway). She, along with her brother Bill (see William Benjamin Smith entry), who was four years younger, lived with their aunt, Mrs. Joseph William Charles—their mother died of tuberculosis in 1899. "Katy" was attractive—but not overly so, as they say—with beautiful green eyes. Outspoken, she wasn't bashful, but neither was she rude. She died tragically of an automobile accident in Wareham, Plymouth County, Massachusetts—the crash left her husband, John Dos Passos, blind in one eye. Katy Dos Passos was buried in Snow Cemetery in Truro, Barnstable County, Massachusetts. The couple had no children.[86]

F. Scott Fitzgerald—"Scott," Author

Novelist, essayist, screenwriter and prolific short story writer Francis Scott Key Fitzgerald (September 24, 1896–December 21, 1940) was best known for his Jazz Age novels, his second of which (*The Beautiful and Damned*) propelled him into the literary spotlight. Success and fortune were his during the 1920s, but it wasn't until after his death that he received acclaim as one of the greatest American writers of the twentieth century. Influenced by the modernist writers and artists of the Lost Generation expatriate community, he frequented Europe and met Ernest Hemingway in Paris in the spring

Arnold W. Gingrich was the editor of and, along with two other publishers, co-founder of *Esquire* magazine. He is pictured here testifying before a committee of the U.S. House of Representatives. *Library of Congress, LC-DIG-hec-25145 (digital file from original negative).*

of 1925. And it was Fitzgerald who convinced Scribner's editor Maxwell Perkins that Hemingway really was the talent people claimed.

By the summer of 1925, Hemingway was on a first-name basis with "Scott" and his wife, Zelda. While Hemingway basked in Scott's unrestrained admiration, he couldn't stand Zelda—"insane" was the descriptor he used in *A Moveable Feast*. The reasons were many, including her willingness to distract her husband from working on his novels—which in the wake of *The Great Gatsby*, Hemingway felt was Fitzgerald's true calling.

The relationship between Hemingway and Fitzgerald was complex, thus the existence of entire books on the topic. Originally good friends—yet if you read their correspondence, Hemingway was a master at throwing darts at Fitzgerald—the relationship slowly deteriorated. Impressed by the writer's work, Hemingway was unimpressed by Scott's lack of self-respect and self-confidence—thus the mastermind behind Jay Gatsby became nothing more than a punching bag. Both Fitzgerald's marriage and his drinking were self-destructive in Hemingway's view. Scott felt Hemingway was overly sensitive to criticism, stubborn and brash. While at times he admired his masculinity, he was repulsed by his unbounded ego.

Fitzgerald was forever a topic of conversation and criticism, thus his inclusion here. As a "frenemy" of Hemingway, he had a standing invitation to attend Mob activities.

Arnold Gingrich—"Arnie," Editor

Arnold Speare Gingrich (December 5, 1903–July 9, 1976) was the editor of and, along with publisher David A. Smart and Henry L. Jackson, co-founder of *Esquire* magazine. Born in Grand Rapids, Michigan, Gingrich was a graduate of the University of Michigan. After honing his skills in the advertising business, it was time to take his boundless creativity further. That was when *Esquire* became his communication dream—it was a forum for his business and editing skills, not to mention his keen eye for literary talent. His roster of contributors included Truman Capote, John Dos Passos, William Faulkner, F. Scott Fitzgerald, Ernest Hemingway, Norman Mailer, and John Steinbeck. And its format, which presented "cheesecake imagery," became a template for the men's magazines of the 1950s. As a Renaissance man, Gingrich was a talented editor, expert fly-fisherman and even an accomplished violinist.

As fate might have it, it was in a New York bookstore owned by Marguerite and Henry Louis Cohn that Gingrich happened to run into Hemingway. Later, Gingrich was smart enough to use the meeting as a reason for contacting Hemingway by mail and offering him an opportunity to contribute to his magazine. The sales pitch, which contained plenty of praise and a promise never to alter an article, struck a nerve. Not thrilled by the standard fee of $250 per story, Hemingway nevertheless accepted the payment. He also promised to write one piece for each of Gingrich's first-year quarterly issues of *Esquire*. Hemingway's first story, a "Cuban Letter" titled "Marlin off the Morro," appeared in the magazine's first issue (October 1933). The magazine, with its notable contributors, was a hit. And the inaugural issue's success persuaded Hemingway to raise his fee to twice the going rate.

Hemingway sent his next contribution, "A Spanish Letter," from Madrid, Spain, on September 25, 1933. The article was published in the second issue on January 1934. Interestingly, the piece arrived in an envelope from the Piggott Land Company—the author was notorious for writing and mailing letters on a variety of letterhead—and he misspelled his editor's name, "Mr. Arnold Gingritch."

As a regular contributor of both nonfiction and fiction to *Esquire*—one of the articles being "The Snows of Kilimanjaro"—Ernest Hemingway appeared in twenty-eight of the first thirty-three issues of the magazine. Hemingway acted as a communication conduit for Gingrich, as the author introduced him to the likes of Theodore Dreiser, Ring Lardner and Ezra Pound. In return, *Esquire* was a channel for Hemingway's ultra-masculine identity.

Ernest Hemingway—"Mahatma," "Old Master," "Old Hem"

The contractor of the Hemingway Mob was a fearless gladiator—the type of man who would rather stare down a charging lion than put a bullet between his eyes—but if he had to do either, so be it. Ernest Hemingway lived hard, worked hard and played even harder. To him, death wasn't an ending, it was simply a byproduct in the manufacture or synthesis of the Hemingway Mythos.

Ernest Hemingway posing with a marlin, Havana Harbor, Cuba, July 1934. *Ernest Hemingway Collection. John F. Kennedy Presidential Library and Museum, Boston.*

Leicester Hemingway—"Baron," Brother

The youngest of Ernest's six siblings, Leicester Clarence Hemingway (April 1, 1915–September 13, 1982), was an author of six books, including *The Sound of the Trumpet* (1953), based on his experiences in France and Germany during World War II. Standing six feet tall and weighing about 180 pounds, he had deep blue eyes and brown hair. Handsome, like all the Hemingway men, he turned many a female head.

In 1961, Leicester published *My Brother, Ernest Hemingway*, a well received and financially successful biography. Similar to his brother, he wrote about fishing and outdoor activities for men's publications. As a diabetic later in life, he faced many a health issue. Leicester Hemingway died of a self-inflicted head wound caused by a handgun at his home in Miami Beach.

*John Herrmann—Writer

John Theodore Herrmann (1900–1959) lived in Paris in the 1920s. As part of its famous expatriate American writers' circle, he befriended John Dos Passos, Ernest Hemingway, Katharine Anne Porter and William Carlos Williams. Herrmann's first novel, *What Happens*, published in Paris, was considered obscene and banned in the United States. In 1932, *Scribner's Magazine* awarded Herrmann a short novel prize—his first national recognition—for "The Big Short Trip." Later, he became associated with the "Ware Group," a covert group of operatives within the U.S. government aiding Soviet intelligence agents. He died in Mexico in April 1959.

*Guy Hickok—"Gros"

Guy Carlton Hickok (1888–1951), born in Trumbull, Ohio, married Mary Elizabeth Chandler (1892–1983) on August 26, 1914, in Michigan. The pair, along with Guy's stepmother, Clara (1868–1949), then moved to New York City, where Guy worked as a silk salesman. It was as a foreign correspondent for the *Brooklyn Daily Eagle* that Guy met Ernest Hemingway in Paris. The pair shared many interests, including boxing. Guy was a handsome man who stood five feet eight inches and weighed a bit under two hundred pounds. It was also while in Paris that Mary and Hadley Hemingway developed a strong bond.

Upon returning to New York, Guy, who was a news editor for the *Voice of America*, and Mary, along with their two children, Robert (1915–1995) and Andrée (1920–2012), eventually found a home in Connecticut.[87]

Harold Key—"Jakie," Charter Boat Captain/Bookkeeper

Born in Key West, Harold "Jakie" Key (February 18, 1890–August 9, 1971) married Ella E. Adams (1888–1947), also of Key West, in 1908. In 1940, the pair, along with their son, daughter and grandson, rented a home at 1026 Varela Street on the island. While Harold, who was short and stout with blue eyes and brown hair, was working as a bookkeeper at that time, he always considered himself a mariner at heart. Later, Captain Key's fishing charter boat *Little Legion/Legion* became known for its record amberjack, kingfish, tarpon and wahoo catches. Key loved running charters because of the great people he met fishing. Similar to other Key West charter boat captains, he took other jobs from May until January to cover his living expenses. Harold "Jakie" Key died in Key West, Florida, when he was eighty-one years old.

Archibald MacLeish—"Archie," "Orchie," Poet

In 1923, Archibald MacLeish left his law firm and moved with his wife to Paris, France, where they joined the community of literary expatriates that included such members as Gertrude Stein and Ernest Hemingway. *Library of Congress, LC-DIG-hec-27379 (digital file from original negative).*

Archibald MacLeish (May 7, 1892–April 20, 1982) was born in Glencoe, Illinois. He attended the Hotchkiss School (1907–11), graduated from Yale University in 1915 and completed a law degree at Harvard in 1919. Like many, his studies were interrupted by World War I. After his enlistment, MacLeish served first as an ambulance driver and later as an artillery officer. Giving up a lucrative career as a trial attorney in Boston, he, along with his wife, Ada Hitchcock MacLeish (1892–1984), moved to Paris in 1923. And it was there that they joined the community of literary expatriates. Not surprisingly, they became part of the famed coterie of kindred spirits hosted by French Riviera residents Gerald and Sara Murphy. Other members of note were Jean Cocteau, John Dos Passos, F. Scott and Zelda Fitzgerald, John O'Hara, Pablo Picasso and Cole Porter.

As one of the most talented poets of the twentieth century, Archibald MacLeish was awarded the Pulitzer Prize for poetry in 1933, 1953 and 1959; Commandeur de la Legion d'honneur in 1946; National Book Award for Poetry in 1953; Bollingen Prize in Poetry in 1953; Tony Award for Best Play in 1959; and the Presidential Medal of Freedom in 1977. Archibald and Ada MacLeish are interred at Pine Grove Cemetery in Conway, Massachusetts.

Ada (Hitchcock) MacLeish—"Ada," Singer

Ada Hitchcock (September 20, 1892–April 29, 1984) was born in Unionville, Connecticut. And it wasn't long before she, and everyone around her, recognized her musical ability—she was a gifted piano player and singer. Ada met Archibald in 1910, when she was attending Westover School (a girls' preparatory academy) in Middlebury, Connecticut. Coincidentally, the school was founded by Mary Robbins Hillard, MacLeish's aunt. Archibald and Ada were married in June 1916.

From their first meeting in Paris during the summer of 1924, until they returned to the United States in 1928, Hemingway enjoyed the company of the couple. From that point forward—and despite quality correspondence—the relationship gradually deteriorated. Granted, ego may have played a part, but Archibald MacLeish was participating in areas, such as the theater, that Ernest Hemingway admittedly knew little about.

Jane Mason

Bright, sexy and stunningly beautiful, Jane Kendall Mason (June 24, 1909–December 28, 1981) was born Jane Coyle. (She took the name Kendall when her mother remarried.) With a talent for sculpting and painting, she studied art at the Briarcliff School in New York. Her perfect milky-white complexion was punctuated by her deep blue eyes. Her strawberry-blonde hair, atop a slender and well-proportioned body, drew onlookers like an Ingres painting (Jean-Auguste-Dominique Ingres). And her relaxed posture suggested that she was aware of her beauty and sexuality—and she was. However, she was spoken for. Jane married George Grant Mason, an executive with Pan American Airways, in Cuba on June 11, 1929. But she later fell in love with Ernest Hemingway, and the pair carried on a sultry and lengthy affair.[88] Ernest and Pauline Hemingway, who met Jane while crossing from Cherbourg to New York aboard the *Île de France*, were introduced to Cuban society by the Masons. At the conclusion of her third divorce, Jane married Arnold Gingrich in 1955. Jane Mason died in Ridgewood, New Jersey, and was buried next to her husband at Saint Thomas Episcopal Church Cemetery in Hancock, Maryland.

Sara and Gerald Murphy—Paris Friends

A provocative beauty, Sara Wiborg (November 7, 1886–October 9, 1975) was as comfortable at a high-society gala as she was on a public beach. A handsome man of medium build, Gerald Murphy (March 26, 1888–October 17, 1964) had blue eyes and light brown hair and was an aesthete. Both hailed from wealthy families. Gerald Cleary Murphy married Sara Sherman Wiborg on December 27, 1915, in New York City. In 1921, the couple moved to Paris to escape the strictures of New York and create the vibrant social life they sought.

Gerald Murphy befriended many creative artists and writers while living in both Paris and the French Riviera—the pair had a flat in Paris and a home at Cap d'Antibes (1917–31). During their years in France, Sara became a good friend of F. Scott Fitzgerald and his wife, Zelda. The Fitzgeralds often vacationed with the Murphys, and the book *Tender Is the Night*, of which Sara was the model for Nicole (Diver), was dedicated to the Murphys.

The Murphys returned to the United States in 1932. Gerald was a painter and later president of the family-owned Mark Cross Company in New York.

Left to right: unidentified man, Eva von Blixen, Pauline and Ernest Hemingway and Baron von Blixen on a dock in Bimini, Bahamas. *Ernest Hemingway Collection. John F. Kennedy Presidential Library and Museum, Boston.*

*Lawrence and Olive Nordquist

Lawrence Walter Nordquist (October 12, 1886–May 17, 1963) and his wife, Olive Ruth Watt Nordquist (January 9, 1902–November 3, 1983), who were married in 1922, owned and operated the L-Bar-T Dude Ranch in Wyoming, east of Yellowstone National Park. After the couple's divorce, Olive owned and operated the Nordquist Cabins and Motor Lodge in Cooke City, Montana. Hemingway's draw to the area was the exhilarating trout fishing along the Clark's Fork River. Both Olive and Lawrence were buried at Riverside Cemetery in Cody, Wyoming.

*Philip Percival—"Pop"

A renowned big-game hunter and talented safari guide in colonial Kenya, Philip Hope Percival (1886–1966) guided the preeminent hunters of his day, including Baron Rothschild, Theodore Roosevelt and Ernest Hemingway. Hemingway even used Percival as the model for Robert Wilson in his masterpiece "The Short Happy Life of Francis Macomber." As a youngster growing up in Northern England, Percival's interest in hunting was ignited by his older brother Blaney, who passed along exciting accounts about his life as a game warden in East Africa. In addition to his association with Hemingway, Percival was artful at teaching and mentoring the finest hunters of his day, including Sydney Downey and Harry Selby. Percival, who had a standing invitation to join the Mob, was often referenced aboard the *Pilar*, thus his inclusion.

*Maxwell Perkins—"Max," Editor

For over thirty years, Maxwell Evarts Perkins (September 20, 1884–June 17, 1947) guided the careers of major literary figures, including F. Scott Fitzgerald, Ernest Hemingway, James Jones, Marjorie Kinnan Rawlings and Thomas Wolfe. From a cub reporter at the *New York Times* in 1907 to a book editor for publisher Charles Scribner's Sons in 1914, he transformed himself into the most influential literary editor of the twentieth century. When Fitzgerald bent Perkins's ear about bringing Hemingway to Scribner's, the editor didn't have to listen, but he did.

Of medium height and weight, Perkins had a long, thin face complemented by striking blue eyes and thick brown hair. Educated at St. Paul School in Concord, New Hampshire, and Harvard College, he was articulate and strategically minded. He and his wife, Louise Saunders Perkins (May 8, 1887–February 21, 1965), were buried at Lakeview Cemetery in New Canaan, Connecticut. The couple had five daughters.

Waldo Peirce—"Don Pico," Artist

Creative, colorful and witty, Waldo Peirce (December 17, 1884–March 8, 1970) made a name for himself as an artist—some critics hailed him as America's answer to Renoir. He served as a volunteer ambulance driver with the American Ambulance Field Service during World War I and was decorated. Peirce, who stood six feet and weighed two hundred pounds, befriended Hemingway in Europe after the war. The pair enjoyed traveling together to various continental locations, Spain in particular. Peirce's creative and unpredictable behavior, or lust for life if you will, fascinated Hemingway. Married multiple times, he seemed to always find solace living in New England. Waldo Peirce died in Newburyport, Massachusetts, and was buried at Mount Hope Cemetery in Bangor, Maine. He remains best known to Hemingway followers as the artist who painted the image of the writer that adorned the cover of *TIME* magazine (October 18, 1937).

Albert Pinder—"Old Bread"

Albert Cole Pinder (November 5, 1892–March 14, 1958), aka "Old Bread," was born and raised in Key West. Both his parents were born in the Bahamas, and the family rented a home in the rear of 419 Margaret Street. James H. Pinder, Albert's father, was a fisherman and delighted when his only son chose the same occupation.[89] Albert married Nellie C. Wells (1897–1980) in 1914. The pair rented an apartment at 522 Margaret Street. At the time, Albert—tall, with a stout build, blue eyes and dark brown hair—was repairing cars and saving money for his future. By 1930, the Pinders owned a home at 1501 Seminary Street, and Albert had finally reached his dream of being a fisherman.

Hemingway and Pinder got along great, primarily because the latter had purchased a large new boat by 1931—Pinder even trusted Ernest behind the wheel of his pleasure craft. By 1935, Hemingway, running short of assistants, was training "Old Bread" as a helmsman for the *Pilar*. As an outstanding carpenter, Pinder also worked for a construction company (1940s). Albert and Nellie Pinder were interred at the Key West Cemetery.

Joseph Stanford Russell—"Josie," "Josie Grunts," Sloppy Joe's Owner

Popular barkeep, rumrunner and fishing guide Joseph "Josie" Stanford Russell (December 9, 1889–June 20, 1941) knew everyone on the island of Key West and every inch of water around it. He married Lulu Russell (1898–1982), and the couple had three children (Anita, Joseph and Edna). Of medium build with blue eyes and light hair, Joseph found success first as a cigar maker and later as a saloon operator. Folks often forget that during Prohibition, Russell ran a small restaurant and speakeasy near the First National Bank.

Joseph and Lulu, along with their first child, lived at 897 Georgia Street. Later, they owned a home at 920 North Beach. Recruited as Hemingway's boat pilot, he became the author's fishing companion for twelve years. Calling him "Josie Grunts," the author used him as the model for Freddy, the owner of Freddy's Bar and captain of the *Queen Conch* in *To Have and Have Not*. He died of a stroke on June 20, 1941, in a Havana hospital. Both Joseph and his wife were buried in Key West Cemetery.

**Arnold Samuelson—"Maestro," "Mice," Writer, Pilar Crew Member*

Having attended the University of Minnesota, Arnold Samuelson (February 6, 1912–September 11, 1981) was in his twenties when he met Hemingway in the summer of 1934. As an aspiring writer, he had yet to find his niche—from newspaperman to harvest hand, he was challenging his skills whenever, and wherever, he could. Admiring Hemingway's work, he showed up on his mentor's doorstep and was offered a job as *Pilar*'s night watchman (and apprentice). Delighted, Samuelson accepted the offer and remained with the author for ten months. Because he could play the violin, his musical interludes aboard the *Pilar* earned him the moniker "Maestro." Struck by the talent of his employee, Hemingway penned an *Esquire* article (October 1935) about his experience with Samuelson and titled it "Monologue to the Maestro: A High Seas Letter."

Eddie Saunders—"Bra," "Braw," Charter Boat Captain

Tall, with a slender build, Edward "Bra" Saunders (February 26, 1876–January 14, 1949) was a successful charter boat fishing captain—his boat *Patrick* landed many a record catch. He spent his teenage years at the family home located at 529 Elizabeth Street. He married Julia Lois Albury (1874–1955) on March 28, 1901, in Key West, and the couple had one child, Annie Marie.[90] In 1940, Edward Saunders and his wife, Julia, along with daughter Annie, were living at 614 Grinnell Street. Both Captain "Braw" Saunders and his wife, Julia L. Saunders, are buried in Key West Cemetery.

Berchland Saunders—"Berge," "Burge,"
Captain Eddie's Half Brother

Berchland R. "Berge" Saunders (June 23, 1897–August 25, 1970) was born in Key West. Growing up at the family home at 908 Eaton Street was competitive, yet he learned much from his siblings. At the age of thirty-six, he married Ruby Susan Bowen (1913–2002) in Miami, where the couple made their home. He was a commercial fisherman. The pair divorced after eight years of marriage. He died at the age of seventy-three and was buried in Miami Memorial Park, Miami, Dade County, Florida.

William Benjamin Smith—"Old Bill," Boyhood Friend

As a boyhood friend of Ernest Hemingway, William B. "Bill" Smith (August 20, 1895–January 25, 1972) shared many great memories with the author. From hiking and fishing to eating and drinking, the pair were inseparable during the mid-1920s. Smith was a sergeant in the U.S. Marine Corps during World War I. By age thirty, he was a salesman living in Oak Park, Illinois. Smith, who stood five feet ten inches with brown hair and blue eyes, was best man at Ernest Hemingway's wedding to his first wife,

Hadley Richardson. Smith's sister Katharine and John Dos Passos married in 1929—as mentioned, she was a school classmate of Hadley Richardson Hemingway. "Old Bill" Smith was buried at Fred Hunter's Hollywood Memorial Gardens West, Hollywood, Florida.[91]

Henry Strater—"Mike," Artist

Henry "Mike" Strater (January 21, 1896–December 21, 1987), born in Louisville, Kentucky, attended Princeton University, where he befriended author F. Scott Fitzgerald. Remaining in France after World War I, Strater studied at the Académie Julian. He met his wife, Margaret Yarnall Conner (1895–1971), at the Philadelphia Academy of Fine Art in 1920. In 1922, Henry Strater met Ernest Hemingway at Ezra Pound's studio. When the author learned that Strater was an artist, loved boxing and served as an ambulance driver during the war, he had a new friend. Of Strater's art, his portraits of Hemingway adorned the author's work, including *In Our Time* (1924) and *A Moveable Feast* (1964). Strater also illustrated first editions of works by Ezra Pound and Archibald MacLeish. He maintained a studio in Ogunquit, Maine, for fifty-five years. It was his portrait of Hemingway that adorned the cover of Carlos Baker's biography of the Nobel-winning writer. Henry "Mike" Strater was buried in First Parish Cemetery, York Village, York County, Maine.

James Bernard Sullivan—"Sully," "J.B.," Machine Shop Owner

"Sully" (June 17, 1886–August 1965), who had a medium build, blue eyes and black hair, was born in Brooklyn, New York. He found his way south thanks to employment by the Flagler Railroad. And by the time World War I rolled around, Sullivan was married and living in Marathon, Florida. Later, he and his wife, Letitia (Louden), a nurse from Ireland, lived in Newport News, Virginia, and Savannah, Georgia, before returning to the Florida Keys. The couple had three daughters.

Employed as a boilermaker, he was one of those guys who loved tinkering with mechanical things. Sully was growing his own machine shop business when he met Ernest Hemingway. At that point, he was living near the corner of Waddell and Alberta Avenues in Key West. Similar to "Georgie" Brooks, Sully soon became a favorite drinking buddy of the

Left to right: James B. Sullivan, unidentified boy and Charles Thompson. Oil painting on the wall is a portrait of Ernest Hemingway. *State Archives of Florida, Florida Memory.*

author. The trio shared wonderful times together, some of which they even remembered. All kidding aside, Sully, Toby Bruce and Joe Russell were the final remaining members of the Mob before Hemingway left the island. J.B. Sullivan died in August 1965.

Charles Phillip Thompson—Entrepreneur

Charles Thompson (November 24, 1898–February 18, 1978) was born in Key West, Florida. As residents of Key West, his family dates back to the 1840s. They ran a number of businesses, including a fish market, hardware store and tackle shop. Growing to a height of six feet one inch, with broad shoulders, Charles weighed in at about two hundred pounds. After the death of his father, Thomas Albury Thompson, in 1906, the youngster lived in Manhattan. Charles attended New York City public schools and then the Mount Pleasant Military School at Ossining-on-the-Hudson, New York. Returning to Key West, he married Lorine G. Epsy Carter (1898–1985) on September 6, 1923.

Ernest took to Charles for his love of hunting and fishing, and the pair often shared Thompson's small outboard motorboat during evening fishing excursions. The scenario worked out well, as any excess catch was purchased by the Thompson fish market. To little surprise, both Pauline and Lorine also formed a close bond. In 1930, the Thompsons rented a house at 1029 Fleming Street. At the advent of World War II, Charles was operating the Thompson Enterprises Inc., located at 816 Caroline Street, and living at 1300 Seminary Street, Key West. Thompson's excursions with

Hemingway went beyond Key West, as the pair hunted elk in Wyoming, rabbit in France and big game in Africa. After lying in a coma for a week, Charles died in Key West in 1978. Both Charles and Lorine Thompson were buried in Key West Cemetery.

Chub Weaver—Ranch Hand and Designated Driver

Leland S. "Chub" Weaver (1900–1974) was a navy veteran of World War I, a graduate of mortuary college (1923) and an experienced wrangler. After his marriage to Laura A. Webber, he worked in a funeral home before heading to the shipyards of Long Beach, California. After serving in World War II, Webber worked as a lineman for an electric company. In addition to driving the Hemingway Ford to Key West from Montana, Webber served as a hunting and fishing guide for the author.

Excursions

By the end of 1928, Hemingway was hooked on Key West. His early excursions with Charles Thompson had him catching barracuda, jack, red snapper and tarpon. He even bragged to Maxwell Perkins that by the end of April he had already caught the largest tarpon (a season's best), sixty-three pounds.[92] Persuading Thompson to leave his hardware store for a weekend in order to take a fishing trip to the Marquesas Keys, halfway to the Dry Tortugas, enhanced the author's excitement. Adding comfort to the situation was hiring Captain Bra Saunders to navigate the delicate Keys while the boys fished. Trolling the deep blue water of the Gulf Stream for marlin and sailfish was a dream come true for Hemingway. As with all the author's dreams, his quest was to see how far he could take it.

Cuba

From Key West, Florida, it is only 106.4 miles as the crow flies to Havana, Cuba. During the administration of President Gerardo Machado, who was elected in 1924, Cuba was enjoying a boom in tourism. American-owned hotels and restaurants seemed to pop up overnight in order to accommodate the influx of tourists. And with the influx of dollars came an increase in hedonistic behavior. It wasn't long before Machado's popularity began to wane.

Ernest Hemingway departed La Rochelle, France, aboard the RMS *Orita* in March 1928 bound for Havana, Cuba. After a layover, he left Havana, Cuba, on April 4, 1928, aboard the RMS *Gove Cobb*, destined for a same-day arrival in Key West. In the United States and other countries, the Wall Street Crash of 1929 led to concern and unrest. Social and political turbulence was rampant during the decade that followed, as the Republic of Cuba could not find a stable form of government.[93]

Ernest Hemingway and Martha Gellhorn, his third wife, purchased a home, Finca Vigía, outside Havana in 1940. The home would last longer than his marriage—the couple divorced in 1945. Ernest Hemingway next married Mary Welsh in 1945, and the couple lived at the Finca. Overlooking the Cuban hillside and recalling his time in Key West, Hemingway penned his famous work *The Old Man and the Sea*, which garnered the author a Pulitzer Prize in 1953 and the Nobel Prize in Literature in 1954.

Dry Tortugas Islands (National Park)

The Dry Tortugas are a small group of islands, located in the Gulf of Mexico at the end of the Florida Keys, about sixty-seven miles west of Key West. The Marquesas Keys, thirty-seven miles west, are the closest islands. The first Europeans to discover the islands were the Spanish in 1513, led by explorer Juan Ponce de León—the archipelago's name derived from the lack of freshwater springs and the presence of turtles. The islands are an unincorporated area of Monroe County and belong to the Lower Keys. With their surrounding waters, they constitute the Dry Tortugas National Park.

The Dry Tortuga islets, or small islands, occupy about 143 acres. They are dynamic and altered by the weather. So, a small islet, little more than a sandbar one day, could disappear the next day yet reappear weeks later. As of 2020, there were seven islets: the three largest are Loggerhead Key (64 acres), Garden Key (42 acres) and Bush Key (about 30 acres), and the remaining four are 4 acres or less. Taking a closer look: Loggerhead Key was the largest and had the highest elevation, ten feet. It was home to the Dry Tortugas lighthouse. Garden Key, a mere two and a half miles east of Loggerhead Key, was known for Fort Jefferson and the inactive Garden Key Lighthouse. Finally, Bush Key, formerly Hog Island, was only a few meters from Garden Key. It was once used to raise hogs to feed the prisoners at Fort Jefferson; the former name died with the pork.

Fort Jefferson and the Dry Tortugas are now part of the Dry Tortugas National Park. The park, accessible only by boat or seaplane, is noted for abundant sea life, tropical bird breeding grounds and colorful coral reefs, not to mention ghosts, ghost ships, shipwrecks and sunken treasure.

Fort Jefferson (Dry Tortugas National Park)

Hoping to suppress piracy in the Caribbean, not to mention a general concern for U.S. shipping in the Gulf, both the army and navy expressed interest in using the Dry Tortugas for defense purposes by the 1840s. Construction of Fort Jefferson (named after Thomas Jefferson, the third U.S. president) began on Garden Key in December 1846.

The new fort was built to maintain the existing Garden Key lighthouse and the lighthouse keeper's cottage. The lighthouse served a vital function in guiding ships through the waters of the Dry Tortugas, so containing it within the structure made sense. Later (1876), a metal light tower was installed atop an adjacent wall of the fort, and the original brick lighthouse tower was taken down (1877).

A massive but unfinished coastal fortress, Fort Jefferson was the largest brick masonry structure—the building covers sixteen acres—in the Americas and was composed of over sixteen million bricks. Highlights of the design: two-tiered casemates (small rooms with embrasures, or small openings, from which guns or missiles can be fired), corner bastions and a granite spiral staircase. The thirteen-acre parade ground contained additional powder magazines, headquarters, a hospital, officer quarters and three large barracks. Since the island lacked fresh water, an innovative system of cisterns was built into the walls of the fort.

At the onset of the Civil War, sixty-two men of the Second U.S. Artillery Regiment, under the command of Major Lewis Golding Arnold, were moved to the fort. The goal was to prevent the fortress from falling into the hands of Rebel forces during its completion.

The Civil War, between the Northern U.S. states (known as the Union) and the Confederate states of the South, began in 1861 and ended in 1865. In September 1861, the first prisoner soldiers, most sentenced by courts-martial, appeared at the fort. President Abraham Lincoln then substituted imprisonment on the Dry Tortugas, in lieu of execution, for those found guilty of desertion. By November 1863, the growing number of military convicts had reached 214; moreover, it would reach 882 prisoners by November 1864. On July 24, 1865, 4 civilian prisoners, Samuel Arnold, Samuel Mudd, Michael O'Laughlen and Edmund Spangler, arrived at the fort. These men were convicted of conspiracy in the assassination of President Abraham Lincoln. In February 1866, after the Civil War, the prisoner population was over 200—a yellow fever epidemic killed many prisoners the following year. Mudd, Arnold and Spangler were pardoned by President Andrew Johnson and released—O'Laughlen died during the epidemic. It should be noted that Dr. Samuel Mudd assisted in caring for many of those suffering from yellow fever.

While the seawall was finally completed in 1872, the War Department was losing patience with the facility. From the frequent hurricanes to yellow fever, it was difficult to maintain Fort Jefferson. The army turned the fortress over to the Marine Hospital Service in 1889, which turned it over to the Navy Department in 1902. They abandoned the property in 1906. Finally, President Franklin D. Roosevelt designated the area as Fort Jefferson National Monument on January 4, 1935. (On October 26, 1992, the Dry Tortugas, including Fort Jefferson, was established as a National Park.)

Marquesas Keys

Part of the Florida Keys, the uninhabited Marquesas Keys are a group of islands located about twenty miles west of Key West. About four miles in diameter, they are largely covered by mangroves and protected as part of the Key West National Wildlife Refuge. As native vegetation, mangroves thrive in salty environments owing to their unique ability to obtain fresh water from salt water—some secrete excess salt through their leaves, while other types can block absorption of salt through their roots. Because they provide nursery areas for fish, crustaceans and shellfish, mangroves are protected under Florida statutes.

The central lagoon of the Marquesas Keys is called Mooney Harbor. The northernmost key or Entrance Key is the largest and known for its strip of sandy beach free of mangrove. It surrounds Mooney Harbor from the north and east. The other named keys to the south were Gull Keys, Mooney Harbor Key and some unnamed keys—Button Island and Round Island are indicated on older charts.

Ernest Hemingway and his sons Patrick "Mouse" and Jack "Bumby" Hemingway, posing with a tuna at the docks in Bimini, Bahamas (another popular excursion). *Ernest Hemingway Collection. John F. Kennedy Presidential Library and Museum, Boston.*

Rebecca Shoal and Light

Located 6.2 miles west of the Marquesas Keys and 31 miles east of the Dry Tortugas is Rebecca Shoal, a treacherous coral bank that once had a light located above it. After failing to maintain a light on the shoal due to severe weather, the U.S. Army erected a lighthouse in 1886. It featured a 1½-story square house set above high pilings—a lower landing deck was removed once the light became automated in 1926. It was demolished in 1953 in favor of a skeletal tower. The last keeper stationed there was Alonzo Baker in 1925. Bad weather often prevented supplies from reaching the lighthouse in a timely manner. While it survived a few hurricanes, it often sustained damage. The closest wreck to the shoal was the Spanish steamer *Valbanera*, which sank 5 miles east during the 1919 Florida Keys Hurricane. It killed 488 people aboard.

SALTWATER GAME FISH PRIZED BY OFFSHORE ANGLERS

What types of fish did Ernest Hemingway's Mob catch? Amberjack (a common game fish), barracuda (always mean and powerful), billfish or marlins/sailfish/swordfish (a Hemingway favorite), bonefish (tough to find), cobia (good eating, prized by sushi restaurants today), dolphin or mahi-mahi or dorado (always popular), grouper (all types), jacks or jack crevalle (strong fighters), kingfish (December–April), mackerel, snook (always hard to find), permit (February–May), red snapper (great eating fish), spotted sea trout, tarpon (tremendous fighting fish but an acquired taste for consumption), tuna and wahoo.

3

IN THE AUTHOR'S FOOTSTEPS

Route One: From Whitehead Street West

Time to walk in the footsteps of Ernest Hemingway. For your convenience, we split the island into three areas, chose some interesting locations and created three routes, with over seventy addresses worth noting:

- Route One—Whitehead Street, traveling southeast (everything west of Whitehead Street)
- Route Two—Duval Street, traveling southeast (everything between Whitehead Street and White Street)
- Route Three—An assortment of Hemingway addresses (east of White Street)

While these routes are in the order the author suggests, only you know and understand what limitations or restraints you are under—or where you choose to begin. Please select the mode of transportation that best suits your needs. Proper planning and preparation on your part will assure that you have a safe and enjoyable experience.

Each route comprises public or commercial locations, along with addresses of interest or reference points applicable to Ernest Hemingway. Please respect all property, be it public or private. For those addresses listed as AOI, or "Address of Interest," they are *strictly* that. Unless something has visibly changed, assume these addresses are private property. Again, if a location is not clearly labeled as public (signs stating admission charge, hours), assume it is private property. Designations are dynamic and have changed throughout history—so too some

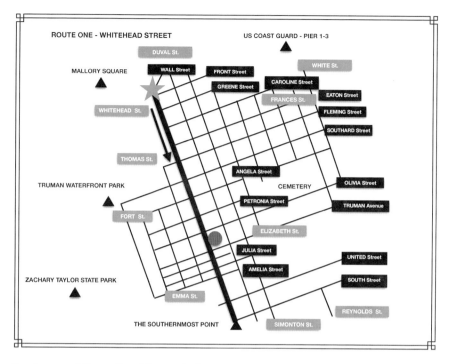

Simple map of Route One. The star indicates a suggested area to begin heading southeast on Whitehead Street. The circle indicates the Hemingway Home and Museum as a reference point.

street names, property lines and numbers. Also be mindful that many older dwellings have long been replaced in whole or in part.

Based on your specific interests or other restrictions—keep in mind your accessibility issues (if any), finances, health, time, transportation and weather—a custom tour might be your best option. For example, you may wish to visit only public locations that do not require an admission charge, such as the Key West Historic Memorial Sculpture Garden or West Martello Fort. Or because of time limitations, you may choose to pick a couple locations from each route. Custom tours are useful for those whose point of origin may be a boat, hotel or even a parking space. For example, if you are parked on Caroline Street, then turn to that section of Route Two and begin there (see appendix street/tour reference).

For many, walking may be a viable option. After a good meal and plenty of digestion time, stretch a bit before putting on your best walking shoes. As you apply the proper sunblock and pick out a suitable hat, pack enough water to remain hydrated. If you plan on visiting outdoor locations, a mosquito repellent is suggested. Knowing that you are in Key West, always have an umbrella handy. Watch your step, as pavement can be uneven, and obey all laws.

No alcohol. Laws prohibit open containers of alcohol on most public beaches, parks and streets. And authorities enforce open container regulations. Yes, this includes Duval Street. Please follow all guidelines with regard to COVID-19, its variants or other viruses. If you are mentally or physically challenged, please contact public attractions in advance to determine accessibility.

In January 2020, the Monroe County Sheriff's Office reported that overall crime in the Florida Keys declined significantly. That said, exercise complete caution when it comes to your safety.[94]

FROM WHITEHEAD STREET WEST

The Key West Aquarium is located on world-famous Mallory Square—home of the nightly Sunset Celebration. Since it rests at the corner of Front and Whitehead Streets in historic Old Town Key West, it makes a good place to begin our first route.

1 Whitehead Street—Key West Aquarium

Opened in 1935, the Key West Aquarium, located at 1 Whitehead Street, is one of Florida's oldest aquariums. Originally an open-air aquarium—Hemingway recalled it as such, along with its "Alamo-style" façade—it was one of the first and largest at the time. As Hemingway had a passion for the water, it is a great introduction to the abundant natural beauty and wildlife unique to this region.

YOU HAVE THE OPTION at this point of continuing on Whitehead Street (distance to next location: 400 feet, 2 minutes by car) or visiting four nearby locations.

Note: Distance to *final* location on Whitehead Street, the Southernmost Point, should you remain on this street is 1.1 miles, 24 minutes on foot, 6 minutes by car.

Opened in 1935, the Key West Aquarium, located at 1 Whitehead Street, is one of Florida's oldest aquariums. *Library of Congress, LC-USF34-026274-D (b&w film nitrate neg.) LC-DIG-fsa-8b36323 (digital file from original neg.).*

• • • • • • • • • • • •

Option: Wall and Front Street

401 Wall (Water) Street—Key West Historic Memorial Sculpture Garden

The perfect way to put a name with a face is touring the Key West Historic Memorial Sculpture Garden. The attraction pays tribute to many of the island's influential residents by combining busts along with commemorative plaques in a spectacular memorial garden setting. Acclaimed sculptor James Martin did a magnificent job on the likenesses, which span a wide range of individuals—from the formerly enslaved Sandy Cornish to author Ernest Hemingway, each has a lifelike quality.

Located on the original shoreline along Wall Street (Water Street), the sculpture garden opened on September 27, 1997, and plans to expand beyond its thirty-nine bronze busts of notable men and women. The Friends of Mallory Square Inc., a not-for-profit Florida corporation, was given the task of raising funds and designing the Memorial Garden.

402 Wall Street—Mallory Steam Line Ticket Office

Located at 402 Wall Street, the Mallory Steam Line Ticket Office offered freight and passenger service from New York, Key West and Galveston. It took an average of four days to make the journey from New York City to Key West. When a ship left New York bound for the island paradise, a tandem ship left Key West for the city, thus sustaining weekly service. More than one member of the Hemingway Mob used the service. This ticket office, rebuilt after the Great Fire in 1886, was relocated to its current position in 1962. It is the last important artifact of the Mallory Ship Line.

AOI: Front and (about 112) Fitzpatrick Streets, Tropical Club

The sign outside the Tropical Club, which no longer stands on the corner of Front and Fitzpatrick Streets, read, "Where good fellows get together." Located a block north of Greene Street, it was a convenient location for the Mob. Altering a quip from Fitzgerald, "A night in the Tropical Club and you'll soon learn why storms are named after people."

281 Front Street—Custom House

It has been a notable landmark on the Key West horizon since it opened in 1891. That was the year architect William Kerr completed the structure. And it was the first important landmark Ernest and Pauline Hemingway entered upon their arrival in Key West. Originally, this unique Richardsonian Romanesque structure was designed to function as Key West's customs office, postal service and district courts—the last met here from its completion until 1932, when the building was transferred to the U.S. Navy.[95]

Today, the Custom House is one of three museums operated by the Key West Art & Historical Society. Since it has hosted many outstanding Hemingway-related exhibits over the years, be sure to inquire about current and future exhibitions.

• • • • • • • • • • • •

205 Whitehead Street—Audubon House and Tropical Gardens

Captain John Huling Geiger made a fortune in the wrecking industry and today remains an excellent example of why Key West was one of the richest cities in the nation in the mid-nineteenth century. The treacherous Florida Keys' shallow offshore reef and shoals, not to mention the currents, were responsible for the riches created for the wrecking industry—after all, one man's misfortune can be another man's fortune. Salvaged cargo was brought into Key West, appraised, auctioned and sold. A wrecking judge then determined the split, or the percentage received by the wreck master (first arrival) and the wrecking crews.

Captain John Geiger (1807–1885) married Lucretia Saunders (1805–1880) on February 25, 1829, in Key West. In the wake of a destructive hurricane that struck Key West in 1846, the Geigers began construction of a new home located at the corner of Whitehead and Greene Streets. The couple, along with their large family (over ten children), found the property perfectly suited for their needs. And the family continued to live at the residence after the death of Captain John H. Geiger in 1885—the last of four generations of Geigers to live in the home was the captain's great-grandson William Bradford Smith. The home gradually fell into disrepair and was even slated for demolition in 1958.

After a two-year restoration, the Audubon House Museum opened in 1960. The museum commemorates Audubon's 1832 visit to Key West and shares his artwork within the Geiger home.

Hemingway would often pass the house—having heard stories of Captain John Geiger, he was well aware of the significance of the property—to and from his Whitehead Street home.

You have the daytime option at this point of continuing on Whitehead Street or taking the Front, Emma and Thomas Streets option (four locations).

(Distance to next Whitehead Street location, Ernest Hemingway Home & Museum: about 0.5 miles, 5 minutes by car.)

• • • • • • • • • • •

Option: Front, Emma and Thomas Streets

This option leads to Blue Heaven Restaurant and Bar. Since the first destination will be closed in the evening, and the other two are only AOI, I recommend taking a cab or driving after sunset to Blue Heaven should you have an interest in that location.

111 Front Street—Truman Little White House

At 111 Front Street, you will find the Harry S Truman Little White House. Designed in 1889, it was built a year later. Since that time, the structure, like many of those at the U.S. Naval Station, has undergone numerous alterations.[96] The original wooden duplex, which contained Quarters A for the base commandant and Quarters B for the paymaster, was converted into a single-family dwelling to house the base commandant (1911). As it was originally waterfront property—that is, until landfill extended the useable property—the sunsets were stunning from the west-facing backyard. Later, additional construction blocked the impressive view from the residence.

Ordered by his personal physician to take a vacation in November 1946, President Harry S Truman altered the face of the U.S. Naval Station, Key West, with his presence; consequently, the winter White House was born. The location proved the perfect solution for Truman, who would spend 175 days, 11 visits, of his presidency in Key West.

It was likely that Hemingway initially visited the home of the base commandant in 1934, in order to receive permission to dock the *Pilar* free of charge in the Key West Navy Yard.[97] As the force stationed at the base had been dramatically reduced, there was plenty of space available at the berthing facilities (submarine piers) adjoining the main ship channel on the western shore of Key West. Hemingway's Whitehead Street home meant *Pilar* was only a few blocks from its captain.

Speaking of presidents: General Dwight D. Eisenhower held a series of meetings (1948–49) that resulted in the creation of the Department of Defense. The president also recuperated from a heart attack here; President John F. Kennedy and British prime minister Harold Macmillan met here in 1961. And the following year, Kennedy made a quick trip here right after the Cuban Missile Crisis. Ernest and Mary Hemingway were invited by President-elect Kennedy to the inauguration on January 19–20, 1961. However, the invitation was declined due the author's failing health. The Truman Annex is both a neighborhood and military installation. (Distance to next location: 900 feet, 2 minutes by car)

AOI: 401 Emma Street—Truman Annex–Marine Hospital

Construction of the old Marine Hospital—at the request of U.S. Navy commodore David Porter—began in 1844. Designed by early American architect Robert Mills, a protégé of Thomas Jefferson, it opened its doors on August 2, 1845. Serving both civilians and military, the facility treated those wounded during the Civil War,

Construction of the old Marine Hospital—at the request of U.S. Navy commodore David Porter—began in 1844. Designed by early American architect Robert Mills, it opened its doors on August 2, 1845. *Library of Congress, HABS FLA,44-KEY,22.*

Spanish American War and both World War I and II. Ernest Hemingway's introduction to the facility came courtesy of a 1930 gunshot wound to his foot. Today, the building has been converted into condominiums. The building has twenty-two units and is called Mills Place. The body of water behind the building, formerly part of the U.S. Naval Station, was where Ernest Hemingway docked *Pilar*. (Distance to next location: 0.2 miles, 2 minutes by car)

AOI: 522 Thomas Street—Pena's Garden of Roses

Using an advertising design that mimicked that of famed illustrator Maxfield Parrish, matchbooks for this popular nightspot proclaimed: "Meet Your Friends at The Garden of Roses Night Club, or Pena's Bar, for 'Old Fashioned Hospitality.'" Albino Pena "Pepe" Morales (1888–1976), along with his wife, Nellie Atchison Morales (1884–1973), looked after Pena's Garden of Roses (located in Bahama Village) over at 522 Thomas Street. The surrounding rose garden's fragrance was welcomed after a long day of work on the docks. It was at this address that Pauline met Martha Gellhorn, a journalist who would soon become the third Mrs. Ernest Hemingway. When the U.S. Navy needed the property during World War II, Pena's Garden of Roses was no longer. As for Morales, he was a successful businessman who owned numerous properties on the island. The couple were buried at Key West Catholic Cemetery.[98] (Distance to next location: 800 feet, 1 minute by car)

729 Thomas and Petronia Streets (Blue Heaven)—Boxing Matches

Every two weeks, the empty lot at the corner of Thomas and Petronia was transformed into an outdoor arena. In anticipation of numerous fight fans, portable wooden bleachers were moved into place. Granted it wasn't Madison Square Garden, but it was affordable entertainment for the small island of Key West. Kermit "Shine" Forbes, one of the talented pugilists who showcased his skills, recalled seeing Hemingway for the first time at the arena. As the author was dressed like a hippie—before anyone really knew what a hippie was—Forbes figured Hemingway was nothing more than a

Every two weeks, the empty lot at the corner of Thomas and Petronia was transformed into an outdoor boxing arena. Not only did Hemingway attend and referee a few bouts, but he also brought his gloves (*pictured here*) along to spar a bit with the boxers before their bout.

stranger trying to pick up some easy cash. After his altercation with Referee Hemingway (see introduction), Forbes thought the police were going to arrest him. But Hemingway immediately stepped in to quell his adversary's discomfort. Any man who had guts enough to take a punch at him, the author believed, was okay in his book.

Jerry Weinberg, the popular Miami promoter, handled some of the shows at the arena. He even took a number of the boxers to Havana for promotions. Earl Adams and Willard Russell were also successful at promoting shows on the island.

Speaking of boxing, Hemingway also attended shows at the American Legion, Cuban Club and Navy Field Arena in Key West.[99] Popular Key West fighters included Phillip "Young Kilbane" Baker, Ruben "KO" Cabrera, Alfred Colebrooks, Oscar "Young" Fernandez (a talented featherweight), Young Figueredo, Willie Jackson, Joe Mills, John Nebo, Pete "Kid Indian" Nebo (a prolific lightweight), Baby Reyes, Mario "Bulldog" Santana, Bobby Waugh and Billy West.[100]

Of all the Key West fighters during this era, the most successful was Pete "Kid Indian" Nebo, aka Pedro Nebot. In 1928, *The Ring* magazine ranked the fighter, of Spanish and Seminole Indian descent, the No. 5 featherweight in the world. On January 30, 1928, Nebo fought Tony Canzoneri to a draw at the Arena in Philadelphia. Later, on February 1934, Nebo lost a unanimous decision to Barney Ross during a World Junior Welterweight title fight at Convention Hall in Kansas City, Missouri.

Today, Blue Heaven Restaurant and Bar is located at this address. And it doesn't hide its fascinating past. For example, the courtyard is still paved with slate pool tabletops—the downstairs was once a billiard hall and ice cream parlor. And a nearby rooster cemetery is a reminder of the popularity of cockfighting. (Distance to next location: 0.2 miles, 2 minutes by car)

• • • • • • • • • • • •

907 Whitehead Street—The Hemingway Home & Museum

The Hemingway Home & Museum, located at 907 Whitehead Street, is Mecca to Hemingway scholars and enthusiasts. The Spanish Colonial–style residence was constructed in 1851 by wealthy marine architect and salvager Asa Tift (1812–1889).[101] No stranger to the weather in Key West, Tift had it built sixteen feet above sea level, with walls made of eighteen-inch-thick limestone. Native rock or white coral stones, hewn from the grounds, were used for construction; consequently, it became one of the few houses on the island with a basement. Tift even went so far as to have durable white pine,

The Hemingway Home and Museum located at 907 Whitehead Street. A view from the south corner. This begins a series of six photos of the property. *Library of Congress, HABS FLA,44-KEY,11.*

The Hemingway Home and Museum located at 907 Whitehead Street. A second-story view of the veranda. *Library of Congress, HABS FLA,44-KEY,11.*

from his native Georgia, shipped to the island for its use in construction. Another notable feature is the wide iron railing porches encircling both floors.

As beautiful as the home sounds, that was not the way Pauline and Ernest found it. In foreclosure and in a state of dilapidation, it was all anyone could do to envision it as anything more than a ruin of the past. Yet Pauline saw its potential and persuaded her wealthy uncle Gus that the $8,000 purchase price was the perfect gift. The title to the home was transferred to Hemingway on April 29, 1931.

Having a significant amount of French and Spanish furniture in storage, Pauline had it shipped from Paris to Key West. The décor of (European) antiques, artwork and animal trophies was unique but reflective of the homeowners. However, when she replaced the home's ceiling fans with Venetian glass chandeliers, more than one guest was shocked—light fixtures did little to cool the house.

As for Ernest, he liked the potential seclusion offered by the one-and-a-half-acre lot. Though he was thrilled that the second story of the carriage house was converted into a writing studio, the thought of his own wine cellar in the basement gave him goosebumps. It was inevitable that as Hemingway's

Left: The Hemingway Home and Museum located at 907 Whitehead Street. Stairs to the basement. *Library of Congress, HABS FLA,44-KEY,11.*

Below: The Hemingway Home and Museum located at 907 Whitehead Street. Dining room looking northeast. *Library of Congress, HABS FLA,44-KEY,11.*

The Hemingway Home and Museum located at 907 Whitehead Street. Master bedroom looking northeast. *Library of Congress, HABS FLA,44-KEY,11.*

fame grew, so too interest in his residence. When his home appeared on a tourist map in 1935, he asked Toby Bruce to build him a brick security wall around the property.[102]

Ernest Hemingway lived happily, not to mention produced some of his finest work, at 907 Whitehead Street in Key West, Florida, from 1931 to 1939. During that time, the home hosted family and friends and even welcomed a few six-toed cats—Hemingway's friend Captain Stanley Dexter gave Hemingway a polydactyl cat named Snowball.

As mentioned, in late 1939, after a visit to Sun Valley, Idaho, he returned to Key West. He hoped to spend time with his sons during the holiday. Anticipating his intentions, Pauline took the boys to New York in advance of his visit. Ernest spent Christmas alone in the house, and on December 26 he packed some of his things and boarded the ferry for Cuba.

Returning in December 1940, Hemingway picked up his sons Patrick and Gregory before everyone departed for Havana on December 23—his ex-wife was in Arkansas. (Note: Guided tours take about 20–30 minutes. Leave yourself plenty of time to enjoy every aspect of the property.)

Pool

It may look ordinary for a Florida property to have a swimming pool. But it was far from common in 1937–38, when Pauline decided to spend $20,000 to install the first in-ground (initially salt water, it was converted to fresh water) pool in Key West. And it was an attempt to save her marriage. She knew how much her husband enjoyed swimming, and if this could distract him from his current love interest, Martha Gellhorn, then so be it. It was a mere coin toss from his writing studio, and that was the reaction of the author upon hearing the price tag. Ernest reached into his pocket and threw a penny at his wife. "Here," he stated, "you might as well have my last cent." Pauline had the penny (a 1934-D Lincoln cent) pressed into concrete under glass next to the pool, where it remains today. According to Ernest's sparring partners, Pauline put the pool where his former boxing ring was located.

Studio

Located on the top floor of an old carriage house, behind the main house on Whitehead Street, was the author's studio. And it was here that Ernest Hemingway found solace, creating many of his finest literary works. From gathering pieces for *Death in the Afternoon* (1932) and *Winner Take Nothing* (1933), to punching or penciling out *The Green Hills of Africa* (1935), *To Have and Have Not* (1937) and *For Whom the Bell Tolls* (1940), this was *his* space.[103] A productive day equated to seven worn-down No. 2 pencils or a couple

Inside Ernest Hemingway's writing studio, located behind his home at 907 Whitehead Street, was the author's creative escape from everyday life.

hundred words on his Royal typewriter. The studio was connected to the master bedroom by a catwalk, so recording an idea was never far away. Sitting among his trophies and acquisitions, not to mention books, provided all the security and inspiration he needed.

Pilar

Hemingway's boat, or customized yacht, was an extension of the author. Having control over his life on land was one thing, but on the water it was another. It opened a whole new world for him, and he enjoyed every second. Whereas *Pilar* is not located at the Hemingway House, nor at the navy yard docks, it was an enormous part of the author's life here and deserves inclusion.

Having spent plenty of time on the water, aboard a variety of boats commanded by the finest mariners, Ernest knew what he wanted in a watercraft. Known for producing exceptional hand-crafted wooden boats, Wheeler Shipyard Inc., at Cropsey Avenue in Brooklyn, became the manufacturer of choice. Hemingway had seen the makers' successful *Playmate* line of pleasure craft and fashioned his thirty-eight-foot version after it.

Having recently returned from a safari in East Africa in the spring of 1934, Hemingway was in New York, or in the neighborhood, you might say. All he needed to place his boat order was $3,000 toward the purchase price. Arnold Gingrich, the aggressive New York publisher, was in the process of building a men's magazine called *Esquire* (1933). And he was smart enough to realize that he needed the perfect contributor, aka Mr. Hemingway. Knowing this, the author accepted a hastily arranged advance against future articles to use as the down payment for his pleasure craft.

As an experienced angler, he requested certain modifications to the vessel, including a live fish well and a large wooden roller to assist in hauling fish aboard over a low-cut stern. A flybridge, or an open deck above the main bridge of the vessel, typically equipped with duplicate controls, was added at a later date. The hull was also reinforced. The boat had two motors: a large Chrysler 75 horsepower for traveling and a Lycoming 40 horsepower for trolling. A key alteration was extra-large fuel tanks (capacity 300 gallons), for obvious reasons—small drums could be stored for an additional 100 gallons.

Pilar slept six comfortably or seven if needed, carried 150 gallons of water for use onboard, was equipped with a spacious galley and could carry 2,400

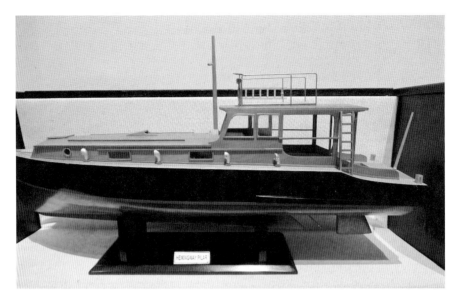

A model of the *Pilar* on display at the Key West Art & Historical Society. Hemingway received permission to dock the watercraft at the Navy Yard located only a few blocks from his home.

pounds of ice. The boat was christened *Pilar*—named after the heroine in *For Whom the Bell Tolls*—it was also Pauline's nickname and the name of a bullfight shrine in Spain. The boat arrived in Miami by rail in May 1934.

After her husband's death, Mary Hemingway had hoped to have *Pilar* towed to sea and sunk off the port of Cojimar, deep into a fishing hole. For it was there, after eighty-four days without taking a fish, the old man had a strike. Unfortunately, Cuban government bureaucracy prevented it.[104]

Pilar remains on display in Cuba at the Museo Ernest Hemingway, located at Finca Vigía, and is now owned by the Cuban government. (Distance to next location: 200 feet, 1 minute by car)

938 Whitehead Street—Key West Lighthouse and Keepers Quarters

Navigating the shallow, reef-laden saltwater of the Florida Keys was dangerous. While that was always clear to the natives, the U.S. Navy really didn't appreciate the challenge until it established a base in Key West in 1823. Lighting the hazardous waters needed more than what could be provided afloat, it required a beacon. The first Key West lighthouse was a sixty-five-foot tower with fifteen lamps and was completed in 1825.

First lit in 1849, the Key West Lighthouse was automated in 1915. It was decommissioned by the Coast Guard in 1969, then turned over to Monroe County. Later, the district leased it to the Key West Arts and Historical Society.

Michael Mabrity was the first keeper, and when he died in 1832, his wife, Barbara, assumed the duties. The Great Havana Hurricane of 1846 destroyed the lighthouse.

Located at 938 Whitehead Street, the current lighthouse was opened in 1848 and first lit in 1849. It was fifty feet tall and stood on ground about fifteen feet above sea level, but eventually it required some modification. Lighting fixtures were replaced or improved, and the height of the tower was raised. The brick-constructed tower was increased to a height of seventy-three feet, and while it was decommissioned by the Coast Guard in 1969, it remains a distinguishing landmark.

Originally built to safeguard the military, the signal light proved invaluable as a landmark to the greatest writer of the twentieth century, who often made the .75-mile evening journey from Sloppy Joe's to his home on Whitehead Street. (Distance to next location: 0.3 miles, 2 minutes by car)

AOI: 1301 Whitehead and United—Ernest and Pauline Hemingway (third home)

A mere .3 miles, or an 8-minute walk, from the Hemingway Home & Museum is the address 1301 Whitehead Street. A two-story single-family home on this site was rented by the Hemingway clan in 1931, while their residence at 907 Whitehead was being renovated. This was Fanny Curry's house, and John and Josie Herrmann lived in it the year before—the address a mere one block from the Southernmost Point and across the street from the gated entrance to officer housing at the Naval Air Station, Truman Annex. The current dwelling at this address, according to public records, was built (all or a portion) from 1910 to 1938.[105] (Distance to next location: 500 feet, 1 minute by car)

Whitehead and South Streets—Southernmost Point Buoy

The large painted concrete buoy at the corner of South and Whitehead Streets was established as a tourist attraction in 1983. And since that time, the inscription on the buoy has undergone editing to reflect the times. Resting at eighteen feet above sea level, it remains one of the most visited and photographed attractions in the United States. Prior to the buoy, an old wood sign stated, "The Southernmost Point, of Southernmost City, Key West, Fla."

Next to the marker is a small concrete telegraph hut that houses an underwater telephone cable that connected Key West to Havana in 1921. In the evenings, Ernest and Pauline often walked east to this point and over to City Beach or South Beach.

Since its advent, the accuracy of the location has always been questioned. Nevertheless, this location is popular and almost always busy. A more southern part of Key West Island exists and is publicly accessible at a beach area of Fort Zachary Taylor Historic State Park (approximately five hundred feet farther south than the Southernmost Point Buoy).[106]

• • • • • • • • • • •

Option: Fort Zachary Taylor State Park

At this point, you have the daytime (only) option of traveling a bit west, then north to the entrance to Fort Zachary Taylor State Park. (Distance: 1.3 miles, 9 minutes by car) Traveling west, once United Street ends, so do the sidewalks. The author believes it is not safe enough for foot traffic. If you insist on walking, consider turning around and heading north on Whitehead Street, then turn west on Truman Avenue. A reminder: the hours are 8:00 a.m. until sundown, and the fort closes at 5:00 p.m.

601 Howard England Way—Fort Zachary Taylor State Park

Fort Zachary Taylor State Park, which now covers a total of fifty-four acres, is a National Historic Landmark—much of the area around the original fort was filled in.[107] Shortly after Florida gained statehood, construction of the fort began (1845). It was slow and arduous because of material shortages, disease and weather. In 1850, the fortress was named after military veteran and twelfth U.S. president Zachary Taylor (1784–1850). Fort Taylor, which took over two decades to complete, remained in Union hands throughout the Civil War, was used during the Spanish-American War and was updated and serviced during World War I, World War II and the Cuban Missile Crisis. By 1947, the army had turned Fort Taylor over to the navy to maintain. Fort Taylor was placed on the National Register of Historic Places in 1971 and, two years later, designated as a National Historic Landmark.

Located near the southern tip of Key West, it has long been a notable landmark. For Hemingway, there were days on the water where it was never a more welcome image.

• • • • • • • • • • • •

4

IN THE AUTHOR'S FOOTSTEPS

Route Two: Duval Street
Between Whitehead Street and White Street

Welcome to the world's longest Main Street, as Duval runs from the Gulf of Mexico to the Atlantic Ocean. This suggested route will begin at the north end of Duval Street and travel south. (Walking south on Duval, visitors will pass 201 Front Street, familiar to most as the boarding station for the Conch Tour Train.) Staying on Duval Street the entire time or combining it with a north–south side street option is up to you. If you are going to remain on Duval Street, an epicenter for the Key West experience, skip the suggested options.

Duval Street may be the most enjoyable mile-long stretch of pavement in the United States. From shopping and souvenir hunting to dining and dancing, visitors rave about the experience. And eighteen buildings, according to a National Parks Service survey, are considered historically significant—this includes Sloppy Joe's. The National Register of Historic Places even designated a six-block area as a historic district—you won't be walking in only Papa's footsteps; you will be stepping on history.[108]

(The distance to the final location on Duval Street, 1400 Duval Street, is 1.2 miles—27 minutes on foot, or 7 minutes by car.)

Before you begin, consider some alternative points of origin. You could begin at the north end of Simonton Street. See Option 1 at the end of the chapter, SIMONTON STREET NORTH–SOUTH OPTION (and Casa Marina Hotel) and travel south, or conduct a short dockside tour at Margaret and Grinnell Streets (Option 2, DOCKSIDE NORTH–SOUTH OPTIONS—MARGARET AND GRINNELL STREETS), before heading back to Duval Street. These optional locations are described at the end of the Duval Route. It's up to you.

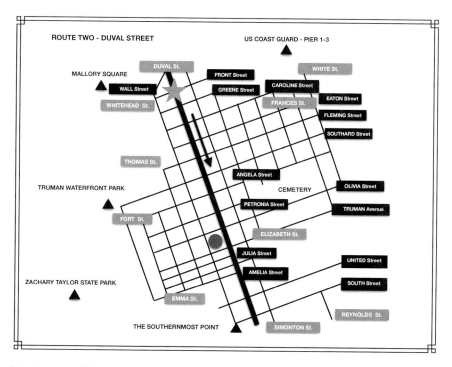

Simple map of Route Two. The star indicates a suggested area to begin heading southeast on Duval Street. The circle indicates the Hemingway Home and Museum as a reference point.

AOI: 114 Duval Street—The Jefferson Hotel

Our first location, as with other addresses along the route, may require a bit of imagination or particular attention to the detail provided, as the large building no longer exists. If you are at the western corner of Front and Duval, you are in front of the Florida First National Bank. Walk southeast down Duval Street, until the bank building ends. An empty lot existed—the current building was built later—before you faced the northeast end of the Jefferson Hotel. As you continue to walk then turn west (facing Hog's Breath Saloon), you are looking at essentially where the Jefferson Hotel property ended). The three-story structure, with tower, had a very large footprint. Currently, a Wells Fargo ATM kiosk is at this address.

On November 5, 1957, the second and third floors of the eighty-year-old landmark were destroyed by fire. Hundreds of men fought the fire for hours but could not save what once stood.

Similar to most Key West establishments, the Jefferson Hotel went through its fair share of architectural changes over the years. The three-story structure eventually shed its tower and attractive porches that faced Duval Street in pursuit of renovation.

The destruction of the warship *Maine* in Santiago Harbor led to a declaration of war by the United States. The war between Spain and the United States—taking place primarily in the Caribbean and the Philippines—became known as the Spanish-American War. It began on April 21, 1898, and ended with an American victory on August 13, 1898. During the war, the hotel was home to correspondents from all over the world. Later, numerous members of the Hemingway Mob had friends and family who stayed at the establishment. Naturally, the hotel drew many nearby businesses—from La Conga Bar to Shorty's, there was always a place to meet—to cater to its clientele. (Distance to next Duval Street location: 350 feet, 2 minutes by car)

· · · · · · · · · · ·

From the northern corner of Duval and Greene Streets, you can glance to your right to see Captain Tony's and to your left to view Old City Hall. Both are Greene Street locations.

Option: Greene Street

428 Greene Street—The Blind Pig/Sloppy Joe's/Captain Tony's

Constructed in the early 1850s, the building on this property has one of the most colorful histories on the island. Yes, it was an icehouse, and it was even a city morgue, but it was during the Spanish-American War that it came into prominence as a telegraph station. Transmitted all over the world from this building was news that the battleship *Maine* had been destroyed (February 1898). Later, it was a cigar factory (1912), bordello and saloon (including the controversial Duval Club owned by Morgan Bird). As a speakeasy, it became extremely popular despite numerous name changes, including the Blind Pig and finally Sloppy Joe's. It specialized in arguing, carousing and gambling; no bottle or skirt was safe in the vicinity.

Joe Russell took the name—adopted from an existing Havana establishment—upon the encouragement of Ernest Hemingway.

Left: The building housing Captain Tony's Saloon has a history as colorful as the town of Key West itself. When first constructed in 1852, 428 Greene Street was an icehouse that doubled as the city morgue.

Below: As the location (*interior view*) of the original Sloppy Joe's, this was where Ernest Hemingway spent some of his evenings between 1933 and 1937. Papa's barstool, along with those of Presidents John F. Kennedy and Harry S Truman, now hangs from the rafters.

And it was on his bar stools that the author spent many of his evenings between 1933 and 1937. When the building's landlord raised the rent one dollar per week, Russell instructed his customers to pick up their drinks, along with everything they could carry, and follow him up the street. The entire bar moved to the current location at 201 Duval Street. And that was exactly how it happened.

Several other saloons landed at the location, but it took developer David Wolkowsky to finally find one with staying power, the Oldest

Bar. In 1958, charter boat captain Tony Tarracino purchased the bar from Wolkowsky and named it Captain Tony's Saloon. This bar was where musician Jimmy Buffett got his start in Key West, and he did more for the bar than any advertisement ever did. Tarracino sold the bar in 1989 but continued to greet fans until his death in November 2008.[109]

AOI: 510 Greene Street—Old City Hall

A wooden-framed city hall was dedicated at 510 Greene Street on July 4, 1876, and burned down in 1886. Russell & Harvey then built a Scott, McDermott & Higgs brick design on the property during the early 1890s. The multifunctional building served a variety of purposes over the years but was best known as housing city offices. Hemingway, who detested politics, entered the building only if he had to.

• • • • • • • • • • •

201 Duval Street—Sloppy Joe's

On May 5, 1937, as though someone had waved a magic wand, there it was. Joe Russell had moved his saloon from its 428 Greene Street location directly into the old Victoria Restaurant building a half a block away. Russell and his patrons picked up their glasses, along with anything they could carry, and headed northeast. Crossing Duval Street, they entered the most convenient wide archway, pulled up a box or a chair and finished their cocktails. It was as though nothing had happened. And with that, Sloppy Joe's, as we are familiar with it today, began another generation. Spacious, the longest bar in town was politely tended by (Al) Skinner, a three-hundred-pound handyman who welcomed visitors with an enormous smile. As Papa's favorite mixologist, Skinner could blend a Papa Dobles (2½ jiggers of white Bacardi rum, the juice from half a grapefruit and two key limes, along with six drops of maraschino) faster than most folks could spell Kilimanjaro or even tell you where the mountain was located. Speaking of drink, Hemingway's usual choice was Teacher's (cheap scotch) and soda.

The history of 201 Duval reads like a Key West history book: At first it was a chandlery (warehouse, 1875), then a laundry (1890). At the turn of the

When Joe Russell officially opened the bar, Hemingway and his Mob were enthusiastic regular customers. In fact, the author once called himself a co-owner or silent partner in the enterprise.

century, it became Restaurant La Liga, then the Duval Restaurant (1913) and next the Cuban-style Victoria Restaurant.

Under Russell's watch, the walls were covered with a variety of items, some relevant, others not so much. From a life-size painting of Jack Dempsey to a 119-pound sailfish landed by Hemingway, there was a story behind every fixture. Likely the most notable item was Erik Smith's mural that hung behind the bar and depicted Skinner, Josie and "Old Hem." At one point, a small stage was erected between the painting and the end of the bar, but it proved far too congested of a space.

The Club Room was a partitioned hideaway in the back of Sloppy Joe's where it was all about gambling. For a period, it was an office that incorporated a window—a set of blinds offering any necessary privacy— that faced out into the bar. It wasn't hard to find, as "CLUB, ROOM" was painted on the window.

On to the story of the porcelain urinal: Joe Russell was renovating the men's room at Sloppy Joe's (Greene Street), and Pauline Hemingway persuaded him to sell her a porcelain urinal so that she could make a fishpond. Once

This was how Sloppy Joe's appeared to Ernest Hemingway in 1938. *Library of Congress, LC-DIG-fsa-8a09357 (digital file from original neg.).*

a price was determined, transportation of the urinal became the next issue. Ernest and Josie waited until the time was right, then carried the urinal to the author's home and set it near Pauline's pool—the gentlemen appeared to be making a statement with its placement. For the plumbing, no easy matter, mind you, Pauline turned to Toby Bruce. It may have sounded like a creative idea, but Pauline quickly learned that when you have cats roaming the property, fish have a shorter lifespan than anticipated. When it was clear the fishpond wasn't going to work out, other ideas were considered. In the end, Bruce managed to design a workable watering trough for the cats.

Once Ernest Hemingway departed the island, Toby Bruce was given the task of packing up his things and finding a home for them. Building wooden boxes, he filled them with everything from pictures and papers to magazines and even fishing equipment. Since Joe Russell owned the house right next to Sloppy Joe's, the items were stored there first, then moved—the homeowner had an opportunity to sell the property—to a locked room in the back of the bar. And there they remained until 1962, when a representative for the Russell family handed the keys to the padlocked door to the author's widow, Mary Hemingway.

As the hours became days and days weeks, Mary, along with Betty and Toby Bruce, sifted through Ernest's relics. Even Toby Bruce couldn't believe how much material he had packed away. While it was easy to get rid of used ticket stubs, newspapers and torn newspaper articles, such was not the case with the original manuscript of *To Have and Have Not* or pieces from *Death in the Afternoon* or *The Fifth Column*. Mary kept all the personal or historically significant items, while the trash was hauled to the city dump. Stan Smith, who owned the bar in 1962, managed to acquire Ernest Hemingway's birth certificate, which was promptly displayed under glass at the historic establishment. (Distance to next Duval Street location: 150 feet, 1 minute by car)

AOI: 215 Duval Street—George Brooks

George Brooks Jr., Hemingway Mob member, once had his office located at this address. It is now home to Shorty's, a popular convenience store. (Distance to next Duval Street location: 90 feet, 1 minute by car)

218 Duval Street—Delmonico Restaurant and Cocktail Lounge

At the Delmonico Restaurant, you always felt like you were in your mother's kitchen and she was whipping up an amazing seafood dish. That was because you could see directly into the kitchen from the wide-open dining area. It was a comfortable setting, as each table for four was set over a white, hand-ironed tablecloth. Large and colorful oil paintings adorned the walls and embellished the Caribbean vibe of the place.

The restaurant was family-owned and operated by Aquilino Lopez (1888–1965) and his wife, Generosa (1890–1989)—both were born in Spain.[110] Lopez's brother-in-law, Jesus Fernandez, ran the kitchen. Lopez described himself as of medium height and build, with dark hair and dark eyes. When Hemingway had an urge to satisfy his well-developed palate, he often turned to the restaurant for their Paella Valenciana.

Never shy about dragging his guests over to the Delmonico (next to the Vic Realty Building), Hemingway was never disappointed with the meal or the price. How can you beat a six-course dinner for fifty cents? And since Hemingway was on Duval Street, after dinner he and the Mob often took in some of the entertainment the thoroughfare had to offer.

Delmonico Restaurant and Cocktail Lounge lived up to advertising: "Fish a specialty, Meals all hours." The proprietors specialized in seafood, arroz con pollo, turtle steak and crawfish enchiladas. It truly was a wonderful dining experience. Today, the address hosts Teasers Gentlemen's Club. (Distance to next Duval Street location: 80 feet, 1 minute by car)

AOI: 227 Duval Street—Watross Boarding House/ The Fogarty Mansion

At one point, 227 Duval Street was the Watross Boarding House. Toby Bruce had a room at this location during the late 1930s.

The Fogarty Mansion

The original house, built by Charles Curry in 1875, was destroyed by fire. Rebuilt in 1887, the house was purchased for his daughter Corinne by her husband, Dr. Joseph Norman Fogarty, as a wedding present. Dr. Fogarty was mayor of Key West when the Overseas Railroad linked the island to the Florida mainland in 1912. As a prominent and wealthy pillar of the community, the family entertained the island's most prestigious residents and guests, including Grover Cleveland, Henry Flagler and William Howard Taft.

Today, it is Fogarty's Restaurant & the Flying Monkeys Saloon. A great stop for a frozen drink or slice of homemade key lime pie.

You have the option of visiting two locations on Caroline Street. (Distance to next Duval Street location: 250 feet, 1 minute by car)

• • • • • • • • • • •

Option: Caroline Street

AOI : 419–421 Caroline Street—Mulberg Chevrolet Company

On this 7,500-plus-square-foot lot, now occupied by a parking lot and a large building (419), once stood the Mulberg Chevrolet Company. This was where Toby Bruce, Hemingway's man Friday, purchased a gray Buick Special Convertible on behalf of the author. Ernest had been eyeing the sporty car for some time but was hesitant to make such a major purchase. Assuring the author that he could obtain a fair price, Bruce bartered successfully and even had a spotlight installed on the vehicle. After all, his employer wasn't shy about a twilight small-game safari.

410 Caroline Street—Key West Heritage House and Robert Frost Cottage (in rear)

Ernest and Pauline Hemingway knew this property as the home of Jessie Porter. A charming and delightful woman, Miss Jessie purchased the home in 1934 intent on restoration. As a fifth-generation Key Wester, she took pride in her heritage and was instrumental in many conservation efforts, including the creation of the historic district.

Along with adding a third floor, porches were affixed for greater social appeal—interaction commonplace in the day. Miss Jessie—who was featured in a 1942 edition of *LIFE* magazine—also added touches such as Dutch door front windows, a turquoise exterior and dining room doors courtesy of the Royal Palm Hotel in Palm Beach. Author Truman Capote, philosopher John Dewey, author John Dos Passos, poet Archibald MacLeish, actor Vincent Price, poet Wallace Stevens, actress Gloria Swanson and novelist Thornton Wilder all lodged at the residence. Key West Heritage House Museum and Robert Frost Cottage (next section) occupy the address today.

Robert Frost Cottage

It was through author Sherwood Anderson, who wrote letters of introduction on behalf of Ernest Hemingway to many literary Americans in Paris, that the Key West author met Ezra Pound. And it was while living in England that Ezra Pound and Robert Frost became good friends. Pound even assisted Frost in promoting and publishing his work.

Poet Robert Frost, a longtime friend of Miss Jessie, found such solace in her garden cottage that he spent at least sixteen winters here as her guest. The poem "The Gift Outright," which he recited at President John F. Kennedy's inauguration, was penned at the site.[111]

As a beloved citizen of Key West, Miss Jessie was instrumental in funding the aquarium, saving many of the island's historic structures and founding the Old Island Restoration Foundation. Born on October 22, 1898, Jessie Porter Kirke Newton lived a fulfilling life, and everyone on the island benefitted by her altruism. She died on February 7, 1979, at age eighty, and was buried at Key West Cemetery.

• • • • • • • • • • •

313 Duval Street—Key West Hospitality League

One of the most beautiful pieces of property in Key West is located at 313 Duval Street. The residence, built by William Curry, Florida's believed first millionaire, was a wedding gift to his son Robert O. Curry. Purchased by the local lodge of Elks (BPOE No. 64) in 1919, it would serve multiple functions in the years ahead.

During the first week of July 1934, the Key West City Council and the Monroe County Board of Commissioners declared a state of local emergency, and the government was essentially bankrupt. The Depression had taken its toll, with an estimated half the population (city and county) on the federal relief rolls. It was hard to believe that this was once (late 1800s) the richest city per capita in the United States. Even the cigar industry, which once employed over two thousand employees in twenty-nine factories, was gone.

In November 1934, a Key West Hospitality League was created and headquartered in this building. The organization's goal was to provide tourists with all the information they needed to have the perfect island visit. Using tools such as the Key West Authority's sixty-seven-page booklet titled *Key West in Transition, A Guide Book for Tourists*, the Hospitality League did an incredible job of fanning the flame of tourism. Not surprisingly, one of the forty-eight tourist attractions on the island was the home of "Ernest Hemingway, the famous author." Today, the address services the Hard Rock Café. (Distance to next Duval Street location: 100 feet, 1 minute by car)

322 Duval Street—The Oldest House

The oldest house in southern Florida was originally located a block or two away on Whitehead Street, but today you will find it at 322 Duval Street, between Caroline and Eaton Streets. Respected for its age, or resiliency if you will, it reflects the master craftsmanship of the era—this courtesy of the skill of Captain Richard Cussans, a ship's carpenter who built the dwelling as though it was his last.

Once moved to its existing location, it was enlarged to four rooms with a center hall to accommodate its next residents, Captain Francis Watlington (1804–1887), his wife, Emeline (1812–1881), and their nine daughters. Watlington served in the Florida House of Representatives from 1858 to 1861. Resigning his office at the outbreak of the Civil War, he joined the Confederate navy in Mobile, Alabama. After the Union seized the city, Cussans surrendered. Once paroled, he returned to Key West, where he died in 1887. Watlington descendants lived in the house until the early 1970s.

Obviously, Hemingway never met Watlington. However, he did hear plenty of stories about him thanks to Hemingway Mob members. One of Watlington's duties for the Customs Office was to oversee the lightships, vessels that were used as floating lighthouses—remember, the Key West Lighthouse wasn't lit until 1849. As the coastal reef locations were notorious for inflicting damage, those unfamiliar with the waters relied on lightships for their safe passage.

For a wonderful glimpse into the past, visit the Oldest House Museum at 322 Duval Street. It is operated by the Old Island Restoration Foundation (OIRF), and the group has done a magnificent job capturing the spirit of old Key West.

YOU HAVE THE OPTION of visiting two locations (AOI) along Eaton Street at this point. However, the walk (clocked at ten minutes) is over a distance of 0.4 miles. (An alternative could be adding them to the Option 2: DOCKSIDE NORTH–SOUTH OPTIONS listed at the end of the Duval Street Route.) (Distance to next Duval Street location: 450 feet, 2 minutes by car)

• • • • • • • • • • •

Option: Eaton Street

AOI: 718 Eaton Street—George Gray Brooks Jr.

George Gray Brooks Jr., barrister and Hemingway Mob member, lived at this address in 1940 with his mother, Julia (Fogarty), a private duty nurse, and grandmother Rosilla. According to city records, the single-family dwelling on this property was built in 1948. (Distance to next Eaton Street location: 800 feet, 1 minute by car)

AOI : 908 Eaton Street—Eddie and Berge (Burge) Saunders

In 1900, the Saunders family address—home to Hemingway Mob members Bra and Berge Saunders—was 908 Eaton Street. According to public records, the dwelling on this property was built in 1943.

• • • • • • • • • • •

430 Duval between Fleming and Eaton Streets—La Concha Key West/KW Colonial Hotel

The grand opening of the seven-story La Concha, Key West's newest hotel, took place on Friday evening, January 22, 1926, and was the social affair of the year. Men and women in formal attire were greeted by troubadours from Spain, along with various other forms of entertainment. While it was no secret that Key West lacked sufficient hotel accommodations, it took developer Carl Aubuchon to fill that need with a first-class operation. Boasting marble floors, private baths, luxurious décor, an elevator and sweeping ocean views, the elegant hotel was unrivaled. Catering to celebrities, dignitaries, industrialists and, naturally, guests of Hemingway's Mob, La Concha was an immediate success. Not a soul balked at the charge of three dollars per night, and many even opted for a steak dinner for an additional thirty-five cents. Everything was fine until the stock market crash in 1929. When the hotel began to struggle it was sold and renamed the Key West Colonial Hotel.

Not surprisingly, over the years it has been recognized in many pieces of literature, including Hemingway's *To Have and Have Not*. In 1947, Tennessee Williams finished writing *A Streetcar Named Desire* at the hotel.

Today, Crowne Plaza Key West–La Concha remains a prime Duval Street location. (Distance to next Duval Street location: 450 feet, 2 minutes by car)

At this juncture you have the option of heading east along an interesting seven-location tour of Fleming Street. From your first stop at 517 Fleming Street until your last location at 1029 Fleming Street, it is an eleven-minute walk over a distance of 0.5 miles.

• • • • • • • • • • • •

Option: Fleming Street

517 Fleming Street—Valladares Book Store

Valladares Book Store, appropriately named after its owner, Leonte Antoniano Valladares (1903–1987), was relatively new when Ernest discovered it. The small wooden structure, formerly a café, sustained a slight seafood fragrance. Nevertheless, the author loved combing over the stacks of books and magazines that could be found everywhere—Valladares was forever stacking, restacking and filing titles. Sharing a love of literature, Ernest and Leonte formed an almost instant bond. And yes, since the author spoke fluent Spanish, it helped. Hemingway even managed to persuade the owner to stock his titles by donating several signed copies of *The Sun Also Rises* and *Men Without Women*.

Leonte Antoniano Valladares was born on February 6, 1903, in Key West, Florida. He married Mirta Lacedonia (1906–1998) in Key West on June 23, 1924. And the couple's son Arthur was born the following year on June 10. Hemingway caught a fancy to the youngster and often kidded with him.

Today, La Petite Grignote, an artisan French bakery, occupies the address. From coffee drinks to baked goods, it is the sister business of La Grignote café, located on 1211 Duval Street. If you still have the book bug, visit Key West Island Bookstore a few doors down. (Distance to next Fleming Street location: 900 feet, 2 minutes by car)

700 Fleming Street—Key West Public Library Branch, Monroe County

From 1915 until 1959, the Key West Woman's Club ran a library on the island.[112] And it was in 1959 that the first county library opened at Fleming and Elizabeth Streets in Key West.

During the 1930s, when Ernest Hemingway prowled Fleming Street, the Monroe County Public Library was not in Key West. But don't let that stop you from noting the presence of the institution and its location.

The founder of the Florida History Room at the library was Betty Bruce, the wife of Toby Bruce, Hemingway's right-hand man. Beloved by everyone on the island, Betty had an eye for Key West history and a desire to preserve it. After Hemingway's death, a stash of documents stored in the back room of Sloppy Joe's was brought to the library for organization. Hemingway's widow, Mary Welsh, sorted through the items and even gave some to the library. A choice donation was a galley, or proof copy, for *To Have and Have Not*, Hemingway's story about Key West in the 1930s. The manuscript contained notations from Hemingway and from his editor, Max Perkins. So, in addition to the Betty Bruce connection to Hemingway, the library became a repository for items related to the author. And there was more to the story.

Long Lost Love

Agnes Hannah von Kurowsky Stanfield (1892–1984) was an attractive American nurse who inspired the character Catherine Barkley in Hemingway's 1929 novel *A Farewell to Arms*. And it wasn't a surprise to those who knew her. Serving in an American Red Cross Army Hospital in Milan, Italy, during World War I, she treated a nineteen-year-old wounded ambulance driver by the name of Ernest Hemingway. The pair fell deeply in love and planned to marry. That was in January 1919. However, on March 7, 1919, Hemingway, now living with his parents in Oak Park, Illinois, received a letter from Agnes informing him that she was engaged to an Italian military officer. The news ripped a hole in Hemingway's heart that many, including his son Jack, believed never healed.

Since a lost love was never easy to forget, Hemingway used fictionalized characters based on Kurowsky in his short stories "A Very Short Story" (1924) and "The Snows of Kilimanjaro" (1936), as well as the aforementioned *A Farewell to Arms*.

Agnes returned to America and worked in New York. She then went on to Romania, returned to New York and headed to Haiti. It was while stationed with the Red Cross in Haiti that she married her first husband, Howard Preston "Pete" Garner, on November 24, 1928. She then divorced and married for the second time to hotel manager William Stanfield in 1934. She remained married to Stanfield until her death on November 25, 1984, at the age of ninety-two.

In the early 1960s, the Stanfield family moved to Key West. And she spent two or three years working in the library. Ernest's brother Leicester met with Agnes in Key West while he was doing research for his book *My Brother, Ernest Hemingway* (1961). (Distance to next Fleming Street location: 700 feet, 1 minute by car)

830 Fleming at Corner of Margaret—Rhoda Baker's Electric Kitchen

A Hemingway Mob favorite was Rhoda "Rutabaga" Baker's Electric Kitchen at 830 Fleming Street. If you wanted a hearty breakfast on the island, especially before a long day on the water, this was it. Home of the twenty-cent morning meal, its décor was nothing to write home about, but that didn't seem to matter much. Eggs any way you like them accompanied by a large selection of sides were a mainstay, as were buttermilk pancakes. "Rutabaga" (1882–1966) as Hemingway called her, hailed from the Bahamas and was married to (William) Stanley Baker (1882–1930). In 1920, the Bakers were living on 624 Ashe Street, but by 1930 they had moved to 826 Fleming Street. Widowed at an early

A Hemingway Mob favorite was Rhoda "Rutabaga" Baker's Electric Kitchen at 830 Fleming. If you wanted a hearty breakfast on the island, especially before a long day on the water, this was it.

age, Rhoda moved in with her daughter Grace Helen Archer at 502 Margaret Street. Both Stanley and Rhoda Baker are buried in the Key West Cemetery.[113]

Today, SALT Island provisions occupies the address. As a purveyor of fine goods handcrafted in and sourced from the Florida Keys, it is worth a visit. (Distance to next Fleming Street location: 150 feet, 1 minute by car)

AOI: 917 Fleming Street—Over-Sea Hotel, later Overseas Hotel

The attractive three-story wood-frame structure that once stood at 917 Fleming Street was known as the Overseas Hotel. Centered above the main entrance was a large pole where a neon sign hung and welcomed occupants. Four columns supported a large covered balcony that adorned the façade of the one-hundred-room complex. There was also a third-story observation deck above the covered balcony. To the left of the main building was a two-story dwelling that was part of the hotel. And to the left of that building was the Over-Sea Restaurant. The guest house quickly became the unofficial headquarters of the Hemingway Mob in the spring of 1928. Guests loved sitting in the wicker rocking chairs on the long front porch (it spanned the main building and both two-story dwellings to its sides), a mere four steps up from the sidewalk, and observing the passersby.

After the old hotel burned in 1967, the remains were carted away. Today, the large footprint of the hotel is occupied by multiple dwellings, but some folks still recall how the hotel looked during the 1950s. (Distance to next Fleming Street location: 500 feet, 1 minute by car)

1015 Fleming Street—Gibson Hotel

The Gibson Hotel, built in 1924, was purchased in 1975 by Mike Eden. And it was Eden who transformed it into one of the most beautiful and accommodating places on the island, Eden House. Taking advantage of the rates that ranged from one to six dollars per day, Hemingway Mob guests enjoyed staying at the Gibson Hotel. (Distance to next Fleming Street location: across the street.)

1016 Fleming Street—Thompson Family Home, Charles Thompson

At the dawn of the twentieth century, Thomas and Mary Thompson were raising their children, one of which was Hemingway Mob member Charles Thompson, at this address. The Inn on Fleming, noted for its Key West charm, now occupies the address—the bed-and-breakfast traces its construction roots to the year 1894. (Distance to next Fleming Street location: 150 feet, 1 minute by car)

AOI: 1029 Fleming Street—Charles and Lorine Thompson

Charles and Lorine Thompson rented a white wood-frame Conch house at this address during the time they met Ernest and Pauline. Not long after, the couple purchased a home at 1300 Seminary Street. A single-family home built in 1938 now occupies the private property. Thompson Enterprises Inc. was located at 816 Caroline Street.

• • • • • • • • • • • •

516 Duval Street—San Carlos Institute

The San Carlos Institute began on November 11, 1871, in a small wooden building on Anne Street. The institution's primary mission was the education and preservation of Cuban cultural values. As one of the nation's first bilingual and integrated schools, it attracted considerable attention. When the original structure burned, it was rebuilt in 1890. Unfortunately, the San Carlos was damaged beyond repair by a hurricane that devastated Key West in 1919. The Republic of Cuba then assisted in efforts to reconstruct the San Carlos. Francisco Centurión, one of Cuba's prominent architects, designed the present two-story building, which incorporates many elements of Cuban architecture. It was opened on October 10, 1924. The institute was visited by many political and intellectual figures of the Cuban Revolution, including José Martí. Ernest Hemingway was aware of the Institute, as were many of his Cuban friends. They often asked the author about it, with some hoping to visit it one day. (Distance to next Duval Street location: 150 feet, 1 minute by car)

527/529 Duval Street—Strand Theater

From the Strand Theater at Times Square in New York (1914) to the Strand Theater on Duval Street in Key West (early 1920s) the Strand name dominated movie palaces built specifically for motion pictures. On February 9, 1933, the front page of the *Key West Citizen* announced the movie version of Ernest Hemingway's famous novel *A Farewell to Arms* would be shown (beginning on February 11) at the Strand Theater. Needless to say, it was a hit.

In a twist of a different sort, the building became a variety of nightclubs before the home of the Ripley's Believe It Or Not Odditorium in 1993. Sold in December 2001 and closed in April 2002, the building has since become a Walgreens. Many of the historic elements of the theater, including its façade, marquee, various aspects of the interior, the lobby tile, marble stairs and wood floors, were thankfully preserved.

You have the option of noting two locations of interest along Southard Street. From Duval Street to 713 Southard Street is a five-minute walk along a distance of 0.2 miles. (Distance to next Duval Street location: 400 feet, 1 minute by car)

On February 9, 1933, the front page of the *Key West Citizen* announced the movie version of his famous novel *A Farewell To Arms* would soon be shown (beginning on February 11) at the Strand Theater.

• • • • • • • • • • • •

Option: Southard Street

AOI: 602 Southard Street—Laura Elizabeth "Betty" Moreno and 610 Southard Street—Benjamin Curry House

Benjamin Curry Jr. was the brother of millionaire William Curry. Purchasing the lot in 1885, he constructed the home at 610 Southard Street. His grandson Benjamin Curry Moreno (1892–1967) and his wife, Rosina Zurhorst Moreno (1895–1988), welcomed their only child, Laura Elizabeth "Betty" Moreno (1918–1994) into this world while living at 602 Southard Street (as you are looking at the front of 610 Southard Street, it is the dwelling to your right). According to records, this dwelling dates to 1901.

By 1930, Benjamin, Rosina and Betty were living at 1101 South Street. Active in the community, Betty was one of the artists who originally designed the Mallory Square renovation, established the history department in the Monroe County library and married Telly Otto "Toby" Bruce. Both Betty and Toby were lifetime friends of Pauline and Ernest Hemingway. Today, town records indicate that the private residence at 610 Southard Street was built in 1938.

AOI: 713 Southard Street—Toby Bruce

Toby and Betty Bruce lived in this single-family private residence that was built in 1909 (renovated in 1975). Always on call to meet the needs of the famous author, Toby Bruce believed the location—0.6 miles or a 13-minute walk—was the perfect distance from his employer.

• • • • • • • • • • •

AT THIS POINT, YOU have the option of visiting the Key West Cemetery along with nearby locations. (Distance to Passover Lane: 0.3 miles, 2 minutes by car, 6 minutes walking) Be advised that most visitors believe a tour through the Key West Cemetery takes about four hours to do justice to this landmark.

• • • • • • • • • • •

Option: Key West Cemetery and Basilica Options (includes Ashe Street)

A quick note on cemetery etiquette: Follow all the posted rules of the cemetery, note and obey the hours, no food or beverages, drive slowly (under five miles per hour) and with care only on the roadway, do not make physical contact with a grave, speak softly, turn off mechanical devices, don't leave trash behind, no pets are allowed on the grounds, monitor and control your children (children under fifteen can be excluded for bad behavior). It is very easy to get hurt in a cemetery if you do not pay attention. Follow all the rules.[114]

701 Passover Lane—Key West Cemetery

Situated on Solares Hill, the highest natural elevation in Key West, an estimated seventy-five thousand people are interred here. The cemetery contains four historic subdivisions: Catholic section, Jewish section, the USS *Maine* Plot and Los Martyrs de Cuba (veterans of the 1868 Cuban revolution).

Founded in 1847, Key West Cemetery is surrounded by five thoroughfares: Angela Street, Frances Street, Olivia Street, Windsor Lane and Passover Lane (Main Gate).[115] Please note that Angela Street is one way traveling southwest, and Olivia Street is one way traveling northeast.

Hemingway Mob members, along with spouses, buried in Key West Cemetery:

Earl Richard Adams | 1902–1993
Richard Hamilton Adams | 1889–1968
Richard Hamilton Adams Jr. | 1938–2003
George G. Brooks | 1905–1969
Elizabeth "Betty" Moreno Bruce | 1918–1994
Telly Otto "Toby" Bruce | 1910–1984
Albert Cole Pinder | 1892–1958
Nellie C. Wells Pinder | 1897–1988
Joseph Stanford "Sloppy Joe" Russell | 1889–1941
Lulu Marie Lopez Russell | 1898–1982
Edward "Bra(w)" Saunders | 1876–1949
Julia Lois Albury Saunders | 1876–1955
Charles P. Thompson | 1898–1978
Lorine C. Thompson | 1898–1985

Since many visitors enjoy finding the graves and then paying their final respects, exact locations will not be given. (Hint: here are a number of internet locations that can be helpful: www.findagrave.com and https://billiongraves.com.

Please also visit http://keywesttravelguide.com, where you can find a Key West Cemetery Map & Self-Guided Tour.)

Founded in 1847, Key West Cemetery is surrounded by five thoroughfares: Angela Street, Frances Street, Olivia Street, Windsor Lane and Passover Lane (Main Gate). Many of the graves feature wonderful sculpture and witty epitaphs.

Many Hemingway Mob members, along with spouses, including Charles and Lorine Thompson, are buried in Key West Cemetery.

In addition to Hemingway Mob members and their families, many friends and associates of the family are buried in Key West Cemetery. For example, some of Hemingway's sparring partners, including Kermit "Shine" Forbes (1914–2000), are also buried here.

AOI: 917 Angela Street—Earl R. Adams

The popular and talented writer Earl R. Adams, a Hemingway Mob member, listed this address as his residence in the 1940 census. The private single-family home was built in 1930.

AOI: 806 Ashe Street—Harold "Jakie" Key

This was the address of Hemingway Mob member Harold "Jakie" Key in 1917. The private single-family home at this address was built in 1928.

1010 Windsor Lane—The Basilica of St. Mary Star of the Sea

St. Mary Star of the Sea is the oldest Roman Catholic parish in South Florida. The spiritual journey of the island—there were numerous attempts to form a permanent mission—can be traced to the eighteenth century. The first Catholic church was dedicated on February 26, 1852, but destroyed by fire in 1901. St. Mary Star of the Sea was built in 1905, and the exterior design reflects the eclectic period of American Victorian architecture. Not only did the exterior impress Pauline and Ernest Hemingway, but its interior elements—Romanesque and early Renaissance characteristics—also reminded them of their days in Europe. Since Ernest converted to Catholicism when he married Pauline Pfeiffer, it also held a special significance: The couple belonged to this church and donated an altar.[116] Most visitors believe the stained-glass window behind the altar depicting the church patroness, St. Mary, Star of the Sea, is the best architectural feature of this beautiful place of worship.

AOI: 1026 Varela Street—Harold "Jakie" Key

In 1940, the Key family (Hemingway Mob member Harold "Jakie" Key) rented a home at this address. According to town records, this home was built in 1938.

• • • • • • • • • • •

AOI: 621 Duval Street—Ramon's Restaurant

Similar to the Delmonico Restaurant, Ramon's was a popular eatery for Hemingway's Mob. Over the years, this location has catered to many businesses and structures. (Distance to next Duval Street location: 0.4 miles, 2 minutes by car)

1111 Duval Street and Amelia (corner)—Cuban Café

Similar to Ramon's, the Cuban Café, built in 1918, was a popular eatery for Hemingway's Mob. While renovation and remodeling have been finely executed, the structure retains much of its original charm. The Cocco and Salem Gallery, which exhibits nationally and internationally known artists, is currently at the location. (Distance to next Duval Street location: 60 feet, 1 minute by car)

1117 Duval Street—The Florence Club/Speakeasy Inn

From 1920 until 1933, you didn't have to remind many folks in Key West that the manufacture and sale of alcohol was against the law. For as long as there were alternatives, nobody cared. And there were, thanks to the rumrunners who made frequent trips to Cuba. One of the most popular rumrunners on the island was Raul Vasquez (1890–1957) who purchased the home at this address in 1920.

One of the reasons he was well liked: the Florence Club, a speakeasy that he ran in the back of his home. Vasquez, who was involved in a few enterprises on the island, was always busy. Thus, the club ran on an honor system. Tabs were kept on a marble slate and often paid when the patron ran out of space next to their name. Surprisingly, the system was a success.

Two things that were unique about the property: ornately designed balustrades (in the shape of bottles) adorn the second-floor balcony—a bit of covert advertising courtesy of a Cuban carpenter—and a basement. Storage below ground level was rare in Key West, but so was the amount of liquor it stored.

Members of the Hemingway Mob, especially island residents during Prohibition, knew Raul Vasquez, or knew of him. And many of those members agreed with Will Rogers, who once said, "Prohibition is better than no liquor at all."

Today, Speakeasy Inn & Rum Bar, an adults-only guesthouse with bar (The Rum Bar), is located at the address. The inn is composed of seven guest rooms. (Distance to next Duval Street location: 0.2 miles, 2 minutes by car)

1400 Duval Street—The Southernmost House

This Queen Anne Victorian–style mansion was built in 1897 by Judge Vinning Harris and his wife, Florida Curry, the youngest daughter of millionaire William Curry. The mansion was designed as a showpiece replete with elegance in the form of spacious rooms, decorative stained glass

Five U.S. presidents have stayed at the Southernmost House. The mansion is located in the upper Duval district and has been converted into a bed and breakfast.

and spectacular ocean vistas. Florida Harris spared no expense in building the house and even hired Thomas Edison to oversee the electrical design and installation. Active socially, the Harris family entertained many of the investors in Henry Flagler's Overseas Railroad to Key West—they also invested in the enterprise.

During Prohibition, the residence was converted to an upscale speakeasy—complete with restaurant, casino and social club. While it didn't always attract a desired clientele, it did attract some, like Ernest Hemingway. Later, the mansion was operated as a popular nightclub, Café Cayo Hueso. Completely renovated for use as a private residence in 1949, it has managed to entertain five American presidents: Harry Truman, Dwight Eisenhower, John Kennedy, Richard Nixon and Jimmy Carter.

Today, the Southernmost House is a popular bed-and-breakfast.

BEFORE FINISHING YOUR TOUR of Duval Street, you have the option of traveling northeast to a South Street location. It is located over 0.5 mile away, or about a 13-minute walk or 3-minute drive.

• • • • • • • • • • •

Option: South Street

AOI: 1100 South Street—Ernest and Pauline Hemingway

In November 1928, Pauline, Patrick, Ernest and his sister Sunny stayed in a small rented home at 1100 South Street. It is at this address where Hemingway finished *A Farewell to Arms*—Sunny was in Key West specifically to type the final manuscript. There are two dwellings on this property—one was built prior to 1926 (back of property), the other circa 1997.

• • • • • • • • • • •

Two Optional Routes

If the Duval Street Route doesn't meet your requirements, you may want to select an alternative option. Option 1 remains on Simonton Street, passing four locations, then ends at Casa Marina Hotel on Reynolds Street. From 314 Simonton Street to 1500 Reynolds Street is a distance of 1.3 miles, a thirty-minute walk or nine-minute drive. If you have completed the Duval Street Route, you could travel one block northeast and return back to your point of origin via Simonton Street (reverse the following route).

If both the Duval Street Route and the Simonton Street option do not meet with your approval, or you would rather linger closer to the water (Gulf of Mexico/Key West Bight), try Option 2. This tour begins at Margaret Street or on the Thompson Docks. It notes four locations on Margaret Street and two on Grinnell Street. From your starting point on Margaret Street to 614 Grinnell Street is a distance of 0.5 miles, or an 11-minute walk. This route ends close (near Angela Street) to the Key West Cemetery.

Option 1. Simonton Street North–South Option (and Casa Marina Hotel)

314 Simonton Street—Trevor & Morris Building

Located at 314 Simonton Street between Eaton and Caroline Streets, the Trevor & Morris Building, aka Trev-Mor Hotel (or Casa Antigua) façade appears much as it did when Ernest and Pauline first strolled into the first-floor Ford car dealership hoping to pick up their Ford roadster. Built in 1919 by Benjamin Trevor and George Morris, the name made sense, as did the location. Recycling bricks from Fort Zachary Taylor, the thirteen-inch walls made the forty-six rooms, on the second and third floors, sound indestructible. It was while waiting for their automobile that Ernest and Pauline stayed in this building owned by the Ford dealership. Finding the atmosphere conducive to his early-morning creativity, Ernest worked diligently at completing *A Farewell to Arms* from his second-story room.

Like many buildings on the island, the property was bought and sold and renovated to meet demand—the first-floor car dealership was transformed into a jazz club. In 1975, the indestructible building was gutted by fire. Rebuilt following the disaster, it featured an open-air three-story interior atrium that made it one of the most unusual properties on the island.

Key West Room Escape, an interactive form of entertainment, is currently located at this address. (Distance to next Simonton Street location: 700 feet, 1 minute by car)

500 Simonton Street—Key West Drug Company Building

Talk about good timing: Colonel Walter C. Maloney arrived in Key West prior to the United States taking possession of the island in the 1820s. Maloney and his descendants began acquiring the island piece by piece, or so it seemed. John Maloney, a surgeon and a member of the third generation of the family in Key West, founded the Key West Drug Store at 500 Simonton Street in 1903. And it was from this building, one of the oldest brick structures in Key West, that Maloney established a hospital that connected to the drugstore—it was created out of need, as an explosion injured numerous workers erecting the Florida East Coast Railroad.[117] Since its construction, the building has been a reminder of the tremendous influence the Maloney-Spottswood family had on the island. Ernest and Pauline Hemingway, like many, took advantage of the Key West Drug Company.

The exterior of the structure today still resembles how it appeared during the 1930s. (Distance to next Simonton Street location: 600 feet, 1 minute by car)

AOI: 605 Simonton Street—Home Appliance Company

This was the address for the Home Appliance Company, which was owned and operated by Toby Bruce. This multiuse building, according to property records, was built in 1948. (Distance to next Simonton Street location: 0.3 miles, 2 minutes by car)

AOI: 1014 Simonton Street—St. Joseph's College for Boys

When Patrick Hemingway turned seven years old, his father took him over to St. Joseph's School at 1014 Simonton Street. The large wooden schoolhouse that was once there is no longer. Later, Patrick's brother Gregory would attend the same school. (Distance to next Simonton Street location: 0.3 miles, 3 minutes by car)

AOI: 1401 Simonton Street—The Santa Maria Motel

Late in July 1960, Ernest Hemingway, along with his fourth and last wife, Mary, made his final trip to Key West. They were accompanied by secretary Valerie Danby-Smith (Valerie would later marry Ernest's son Gregory). Toby Bruce quietly arranged for the noted author to lodge briefly at the Santa Maria Motel at 1401 Simonton Street.

At this point you have options: You can head west on Truman Avenue (Route 1), for one block, then take Duval Street north back to your point of origin; or, travel 0.4 miles to the Casa Marina Hotel—about a two-minute drive.[118]

1500 Reynolds Street—Casa Marina Hotel Key West

Conceived by Standard Oil and railroad tycoon Henry M. Flagler, visionary developer of the Florida Keys Over-Sea Railroad, it made sense: a luxurious resort to cater to the wealthy and tired travelers who made the journey from the Florida mainland all the way to Key West. But after completing his railroad in 1912, Flagler died the following year. Thankfully, his proposition did not die with him.

Enter Louis P. Schutt, a trusted aide of Flagler, who understood the vision of his friend and could bring the project to its fruition. Thomas Hastings and John M. Carrere, who also designed the New York Public Library and the Metropolitan Opera House, worked with Schutt and shared his attention to detail.

Opened on January 1, 1921, La Casa Marina, which means "the house by the sea," would be the latest addition to the chain of famous hotels operated by the Florida East Coast Hotel Company. *Lakeland Evening Telegram* noted:

> *It is under the management of L.P. Schutt, for a number of years in charge of the Long Key Fishing Camp. In the summer he operates an inn in the mountains of New York. This new hotel of the Flagler system, with accommodations for 300 guests, gives Key West an up-to-the-minute hotel, equipped with every modern feature. It will prove an inviting place for the passengers to and from Havana to stop and inspect the world's greatest cigar factories, and the tremendous sponge, shrimp, turtle and other fishing for which Key West is known the world over. La Casa Marina was particularly planned to suit the climatic conditions prevailing at the Island City. Almost every apartment has a marine view. It will be operated on the European plan, and will be kept up to the high standard which distinguishes the other hotels of this company.*[119]

Attention to detail was what separated this hotel from the competition. From the Oriental rugs spread across the glimmering hardwood floors to the black-and-silver cypress paneling in the public rooms, guests marveled at their surroundings. Every piece of furniture was specifically designed for the hotel. It was luxury at its finest. President Warren G. Harding was delighted to be the first U.S. president to enter the La Casa Marina, but he was far from the last. President Harry S Truman gave a dinner party for five hundred guests in the ballroom. Speaking of Truman, during World War II, the U.S. Navy bought the hotel and converted it to officers' quarters. A new owner reopened the resort after the war and began a new phase of its fascinating history.

In addition to U.S. presidents, the hotel has welcomed renowned guests: merchant John Jacob Astor, industrialist and philanthropist Andrew Carnegie, poet Robert Frost, actor Cary Grant, entertainer Al Jolson, actor Gregory Peck, poet Wallace Stevens, conductor John Philip Sousa, crooner Rudy Vallée and Ernest Hemingway.[120]

Route Two—Duval Street—Option 2: This route begins at 200 Margaret Street or what was often referred to as the "Thompson Docks." For years, this area quartered some of the finest seamen on the island.

OPTION 2. DOCKSIDE NORTH–SOUTH OPTIONS— MARGARET AND GRINNELL STREETS

200 Margaret Street—Thompson Docks

The name Thompson carried considerable weight in Key West, as well it should. John L. Thompson (1824–1900) married Clementine G. Sawyer Thompson (1834–1900), and the couple had two sons: Thomas Albury Thompson (1854–1906) and Philip E. Thompson (1862–1897). Thomas had three sons—Norberg (1884–1951), Karl (1887–1972) and Charles (1898–1978)—along with one daughter, Marietta "Etta" (1896–1956).[121] It wasn't long before the three enterprising brothers owned businesses catering to the fishing industry, including a hardware store, icehouse, tackle shop, warehouse and even a cigar box factory. Later, they dominated the sea turtle industry and had their own canning company.

Located at the north end of Margaret Street, on Thompson's pier in this historic seaport area, is the Thompson Fish House. It once had a submerged wooden cage suspended beneath the building that housed exotic fish and maritime specimens. Caught by local fishermen, these specimens were sold to aquariums or research facilities.

Ernest Hemingway spent many a magic moment at this location. If his spirit exists anyplace on this island, besides his home, it is likely here. (Distance to next Margaret Street location: 100 feet, 1 minute by car)

231 Margaret Street—Turtle Kraals Restaurant/Half Shell Raw Bar

At a thirteen-cent admission, Turtle Kraals (Thompson owned) was the seaport's first attraction. Visitors from all over the globe could witness the turtle trawlers unloading their cargo for market. Captured turtles, some weighing three hundred pounds, were slid across the pier on their backs and lowered down a steep ramp into the kraal.

Today, the address is home to two restaurants, Turtle Kraals (recently closed) and Half Shell Raw Bar, home to the best oyster sampler platter (two oysters Rockefeller, two andouille oysters and two garlic cream oysters) on the island. (Distance to next Margaret Street location: 900 feet, 2 minutes by car)

AOI: 419 Margaret Street—Albert "Old Bread" Pinder

The Pinder family home where Hemingway Mob member Albert "Old Bread" Pinder spent his childhood. (Distance to next Margaret Street location: 600 feet, 1 minute by car)

AOI: 522 Margaret Street—Albert "Old Bread" Pinder

Hemingway Mob member Albert Pinder and his wife, Nellie, rented an apartment at this location. This property (The Historic Chavez House) is listed in the National Register of Historic Places. The single-family dwelling (also a guest cottage) on this property, according to city records, was built in 1870. (Distance from 522 Margaret Street to 412 Grinnell Street: 0.2 miles 2 minutes by car)

AOI: 412 Grinnell Street—Richard Hamilton Adams

Residence of Hemingway Mob members Richard "Sacka Ham" Hamilton Adams and his son Richard Hamilton Adams Jr. The private single-family home at this address was built in 1933. (Distance to next Grinnell Street location: 900 feet, 2 minutes by car)

AOI: 614 Grinnell Street—Edward "Bra(w)" Saunders

Residence of Hemingway Mob member Eddie "Bra(w)" Saunders. This stunning private single-family home is full of charm, ambiance and history.

5

IN THE AUTHOR'S FOOTSTEPS

Route Three: Assorted Locations, From White Street East

From White Street traveling primarily eastward, here is a selection of locations that you may find intriguing. Unlike the previous two Old Town routes—that take place on, or off, a central street—these locations are scattered in various neighborhoods. Since some of the locations are a substantial distance apart, you may want to select only a few to satisfy your interest.

What better place to start this route than in the prestigious neighborhood known as the Meadows and the residence of Hemingway Mob member John Dos Passos? This historic property is listed in the National Register of Historic Places.

AOI: 1401 Pine Street—John Dos Passos

In 1934, John Dos Passos resided at 1401 Pine Street. The lot, which rests on the corner of Pine and Florida Streets, is over three thousand square feet. According to town records, this three-story updated private residence was built in 1938. The dwelling has preserved much of its original charm and is a neighborhood showpiece.

John Dos Passos completed his popular novel *Manhattan Transfer* (1925), a pamphlet called *Facing the Chair* (1927) and his travel memoir *Orient Express* (1927) before turning his attention to Key West. By 1928, he had known Hemingway for over a decade, and both had shared numerous adventures.

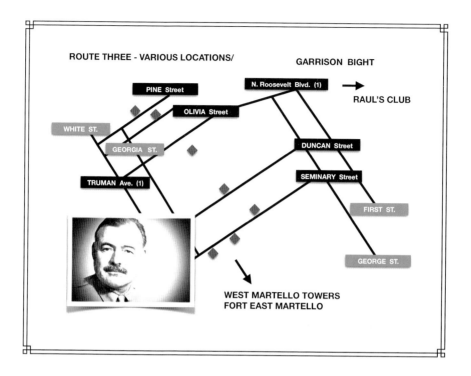

ROUTE THREE - VARIOUS LOCATIONS/

GARRISON BIGHT

RAUL'S CLUB

PINE Street

N. Roosevelt Blvd. (1)

OLIVIA Street

WHITE ST.

GEORGIA ST.

DUNCAN Street

SEMINARY Street

TRUMAN Ave. (1)

FIRST ST.

GEORGE ST.

WEST MARTELLO TOWERS
FORT EAST MARTELLO

ROUTE THREE - FROM WHITE STREET EAST

AOI – Address of Interest: 1401 Pine Street - John Dos Passos

AOI – Address of Interest: 1411 Olivia Street - Joseph Russell

AOI – Address of Interest: 1431 Duncan Street - Tennessee Williams Home

AOI – Address of Interest: About 3500 S. Roosevelt Blvd. - Raul's Club

AOI – Address of Interest: Pearl Street – Hemingway Home

AOI – Address of Interest: 1220 Seminary Street - Henry H. Taylor, Jr.

AOI – Address of Interest: 1300 Seminary Street - Charles & Lorine Thompson

AOI – Address of Interest: 1501 Seminary Street - Albert & Nellie Pinder

1100 Atlantic Blvd (A1A) - West Martello Towers
3501 S. Roosevelt Blvd. - Fort East Martello (Museum)

Previous, top: Route Three—Various locations: Eight "Addresses of Interest," along with both West Martello Towers and Fort East Martello, are included on this route. The diamond shapes indicate the points of interest minus Raul's Club and both Martello locations.

Previous, bottom: A checklist of Route Three locations. These points are primarily "Addresses of Interest" and far more convenient to those residing east of White Street. Unlike the previous routes, these locations are not in close proximity to one another.

Left: In 1934, John Dos Pasos resided at 1401 Pine Street. The historic property is listed in the National Register of Historic Places.

Often recalled was their 1935 trip to Bimini. Aboard *Pilar*, Dos Passos filmed Ernest shooting himself in both legs while trying to kill a gaffed shark.

The friendship between Dos Passos and Hemingway, a contrast of personalities, came to an end during the Spanish Civil War. Dos Passos was a lifelong political activist, while Hemingway typically avoided political movements. (Distance to next location: 423 feet, 1 minute by car)

AOI: 1411 Olivia Street—Joseph Russell

"Josie" Russell, perhaps the most popular of all Hemingway Mob members, led a fascinating life. He and his wife, Lulu Russell, along with their family, rented a house (it no longer stands) at this address in 1920. The private single-family home at this address was built in 1938. (Distance to next location: 0.4. miles, 3 minutes by car)

Tennessee Williams visited and lived in Key West from 1941 until his death in 1983. Establishing residence in 1949, he bought the house at 1431 Duncan Street in 1950.

AOI: 1431 Duncan Street—Tennessee Williams Home

Without question, Thomas Lanier Williams III, aka Tennessee Williams, was one of the greatest twentieth-century American playwrights. His works include *The Glass Menagerie*, *A Streetcar Named Desire* and *Cat on a Hot Tin Roof*— all classics of the American stage. Williams was influenced by many poets and writers, including Anton Chekhov, Hart Crane, William Faulkner, James Joyce, D.H. Lawrence and Ernest Hemingway, and the success of *A Streetcar Named Desire* (1947) secured his reputation as an eminent dramatist.

Tennessee Williams lived in Key West, or visited, from 1941 until his death in 1983. Establishing residence in 1949, he bought the house at 1431 Duncan Street the following year. Built in 1933, it rests on a sizable lot (nine thousand square feet). In addition to his Key West home, Williams maintained an apartment in Manhattan at 235 East 58th Street.

Tennessee Williams Meets Ernest Hemingway

A common question with Key West visitors has always been: Did Tennessee Williams ever meet Ernest Hemingway? The answer is yes, but not in the

Tennessee Williams walking to a service for Dylan Thomas (1953). This photo was taken a few months after the premiere of his play *Camino Real. Library of Congress, LC-USZ62-115075 (b&w film copy neg.).*

location you might think. The pair met in March 1959, in Havana, Cuba. The meeting was arranged by English theater critic and writer Kenneth Tynan, who was in Cuba to conduct an interview with Fidel Castro. Tynan arranged a luncheon date with Hemingway at the Floridita, and Williams tagged along. Nervous, Williams turned to the common denominator, which were acquaintances. He spoke to meeting bullfighter Antonio Ordonez in Spain and even Pauline in Key West. However, the conversation waned and was awkward at best. Hemingway was not impressed by the playwright, and the playwright was not impressed with the manner in which he conducted himself. (Distance to next location: 2.5 miles, 9 minutes by car)

Note: If you skip the next location, Raul's Club, the distance to the next location, or Pearl Street (general area), is: 450 feet, 1 minute by car)

AOI: About 3500 South Roosevelt Boulevard—Raul's Club (Raul Vasquez)/Club Mirimar

Raul's Club on South Roosevelt Boulevard (about 3500, it no longer exists), despite the distance from Old Town, was a favorite of Hemingway's Mob. By the time Vasquez opened his club, he was already a legendary rumrunner and loved entertaining patrons with his tales or taking them out to the pool behind the nightclub and feeding a variety of fish by hand. It was a lavish club that had an enormous dance floor where patrons could swing to impressive entertainment. The entrance to the venue had an overhang supported by two large pointed columns that read "RAUL'S CLUB" in a vertical format. The bar, which had an African feel, thanks to the furnishings and large mural (complete with elephant) behind it, seated over a dozen comfortably.
   (Distance to next area: 2.5 miles, 8 minutes by car)

AOI: Pearl Street—Hemingway Home

In February 1930, Ernest, Pauline, Patrick and Sunny (whose stay was brief) arrived in Key West from Paris. Lorine Thompson had found them a spacious single-family home (it no longer exists) over on Pearl Street. The rent was reasonable, and it was near the Casino. (This section of Pearl Street was taken for construction of Horace Obryant Middle School, 1105 Leon Street.) Regardless of the location—a good walk from Old Town—Hemingway maintained his island contacts. Anticipating another run to the Dry Tortugas, he even rented a large cabin cruiser. (Distance to next location: 0.4 miles, 3 minutes by car)

In February 1930, Ernest, Pauline, Patrick and Sunny (who would briefly stay) arrived back in Key West from Paris. Lorine Thompson had found them a spacious single-family home (it no longer exists) over on Pearl Street. This popular Lloyd Arnold photograph adorned the back cover of *For Whom the Bell Tolls. Ernest Hemingway Collection. John F. Kennedy Presidential Library and Museum, Boston.*

AOI: 1220 Seminary Street—Henry H. Taylor Jr.

Graduating from the University of Florida and Law School in 1935, Henry Hamilton Taylor Jr. (1912–2011) joined his father's law practice, McCaskill, Taylor & McCaskill (124 Duval). Arguing his first case in front of the Florida Supreme Court in 1936, he practiced in both Miami and Key West. A major in the U.S. Army during World War II, he served his country with distinction. Starting his own firm, Taylor, Brion, Buker, & Greene, he represented many prestigious companies and individuals, including Ernest Hemingway and later Hemingway's wife. Renting a dwelling at this address, Henry Taylor conducted aspects of his private practice within its walls. (Distance to next location: 600 feet, 1 minute by car)

AOI: 1300 Seminary Street—Charles and Lorine Thompson

Charles and Lorine Thompson, having left the family home at 1029 Fleming Street (circa 1934), purchased a house at 1300 Seminary Street and lived there during the World War II years. Their stone home no longer exists. Hemingway referred to the area as "Fisherman's Row," as it was a few blocks south of Garrison Bight. The private single-family home at this address is believed to have been built in 1999. (Distance to next location: 600 feet, 1 minute by car)

AOI: 1501 Seminary Street—Albert and Nellie Pinder

Former address of Hemingway Mob member Albert "Old Bread" Pinder. The home no longer exists. Albert and Nellie, along with daughter Rose and uncle James Knowles, resided here in 1930. Later, they lived along the Oversea Highway. The private single-family home at this address was built in 1943. (Distance to Atlantic Boulevard location: 0.7 miles, 4 minutes by car)

1100 Atlantic Boulevard (A1A)—West Martello Towers

3501 South Roosevelt Boulevard—Fort East Martello (Museum)

The East and West Martello Towers were built by the Union military in 1862 during the American Civil War (1861–1865). The primary objective for both was to provide defensive support to Fort Zachary Taylor. The West Martello Tower was built about one and a half miles east of Fort Taylor, while the East Martello Tower was located two miles east of the West Tower. No armaments were ever installed at the towers, and construction was suspended in 1866.

Of the two fortifications, the East Martello Tower has retained most of its original appearance. Today, East Martello is operated as a museum with a large collection of Key West artifacts, historical records and military memorabilia, including Civil War objects. As the towers were never involved in a battle, the visible damage to the West Martello Tower occurred when it was used by the U.S. Navy for target practice. West Martello Tower is a

The East and West Martello Towers were built by the Union military in 1862, during the American Civil War (1861–1865). The primary objective for both was to provide defensive support to Fort Zachary Taylor. A view of the East Mortello Tower. *Library of Congress, LC-DIG-fsa-8b36326 (digital file from original neg.)*

national historic site and home to the Joe Allen Garden Center and Key West Garden Club.[122]

When Captain Hemingway was behind the wheel of the *Pilar*, both notable landmarks were a welcome vision. At one point in time, there was talk of displaying Ernest Hemingway's taxidermy mounted animals at the museum. (Distance from 1100 Atlantic Boulevard to 3501 South Roosevelt Boulevard: 2.2 miles, 6 minutes by car)

6

THE KEY WEST WRITTEN WORK
OF ERNEST HEMINGWAY, 1928-1940

Seeking answers, yet unsure of the questions, people were drawn to Key West for reasons they couldn't even fathom. Throughout its rich history, Key West has attracted artists, entrepreneurs, fisherman, musicians, pirates, ship wreckers, smugglers and even thrill-seekers. Arriving via every mode of conceivable transportation, many were seeking something. Be it straightforward, such as a reprieve from the cold weather, or more complex, like finding themselves, they sought solutions. Since creativity, and even productivity, have always found a home on the island—or at least since 1928—many were convinced there must be a reason. Perhaps some sort of magic. To find it, they believed, would provide them the answer they were looking for.

Ernest Hemingway found what he was looking for on the island: The environment stimulated his creativity and enhanced his efficiency. Granted, the inspiration for some of his work came from other places, but the bulk of the work was completed in Key West. All the ingredients necessary to do so, at least from his perspective, were found in this tropical paradise.

As impressive as the quality of Hemingway's work was during this time, so too the level of productivity. A quick glance at a bulk, but not all, of his written output during this time supports this claim.

1929

A Farewell to Arms, published on September 27, 1929, was the author's first conspicuous success in terms of sales.[123] The novel, set against the backdrop of World War I, describes a love affair between the expatriate Frederic Henry, serving in the ambulance corps of the Italian army, and an English nurse, Catherine Barkley. As Ernest Hemingway's first bestseller, its publication drew considerable interest from his peers. The book was written at various locations, including Arkansas, Florida, Kansas and Wyoming. The author struggled with the ending, to the tune of between thirty-nine and forty-seven variations. With regard to periodical contributions (articles, poems or short stories), Hemingway contributed a poem, "Valentine," to *Little Review*.

Set against the backdrop of World War I, *A Farewell to Arms* drew from Ernest Hemingway's personal experience serving in the ambulance corps. The author is pictured here in uniform, 1918. *Ernest Hemingway Collection. John F. Kennedy Presidential Library and Museum, Boston.*

1930

The Scribner reissue of the Boni & Liveright edition of *In Our Time* (1925), complete with a new introduction by Hemingway, was published on October 24, 1930. With regard to periodical contributions (articles, poems or short stories), Hemingway penned an article for *Fortune*, "Bullfighting, Sport and Industry," and contributed a short story to *Scribner's Magazine*. The author also wrote an introduction that appeared in *Kiki's Memoirs*, by Edward Titus.

1931

Hemingway's heart was in his bullfighting book, along with the birth of his next child. With regard to periodical contributions (articles, poems or short stories), Hemingway contributed a short story, "The Sea Change," to *This Quarter*.

1932

Hemingway's nonfiction book about bullfighting was titled *Death in the Afternoon*, and it was published on September 23, 1932. The book, an examination of the history and Spanish traditions of bullfighting, was also a study on the nature of fear and chivalry. Three main sections—text, eighty-one photographs and glossary—introduced the reader to the art of Spanish bullfighting. Scribner's decided on a short, but expensive, print run of 10,300 copies. The stunning color dust jacket features a facsimile of *Toros* by artist Roberto Domingo on the cover. Other segments include "Some Reactions of a Few Individuals to the Integral Spanish Bullfight"; "A Short Estimate of the American, Sidney Franklin, as a Matador" and "Date of Which Bullfights Will Ordinarily Be Held in Spain, France, Mexico and Central and South America."[124] With regard to periodical contributions (articles, poems or short stories), Hemingway contributed a short story to *Cosmopolitan*, "After the Storm."[125]

Hemingway's nonfiction book about bullfighting was titled *Death in the Afternoon* and published on September 23, 1932. *Library of Congress, LC-DIG-agc-7a04308 (digital file from original neg.).*

1933

Published on October 27, 1933, *Winner Take Nothing* was a collection of fourteen short stories. Six of the fourteen stories were new: "The Light of the World," "A Way You'll Never Be," "The Mother of a Queen," "One Reader Writes," "A Day's Wait" and "Fathers and Sons." It was believed to have an initial print run of approximately twenty thousand copies. With regard to periodical contributions (articles, poems or short stories): Hemingway's thirty-one contributions (from 1933 until 1939) to *Esquire* began with "Marlin off the Morro," in the magazine's premier issue (Vol. 1, Autumn 1933). The author also contributed his final three short stories to *Scribner's Magazine*.

1934

Periodical contributions (articles, poems or short stories) permeated the author's schedule during the year: Hemingway turned out nine contributions to *Esquire*, including "Defense of Dirty Words."[126] *Cosmopolitan* was thrilled with the author's story "One Trip Across," to such an extent that the magazine purchased it for $5,500 and printed it in April. This was the story that introduced the Depression-era character Harry Morgan, who resurfaces in *To Have and Have Not*.

1935

Publicity, which early in the year focused on the film adaption of *A Farewell to Arms*, next examined the author's landing of a 786-pound mako shark on rod and reel near Bimini, before finally turning to his written work with the publication of *The Green Hills of Africa* on October 25. Whereas its serialization in *Scribner's Magazine* was welcome, the book was a disappointment. The Depression—which affected sales of *Death in the Afternoon*—also contributed to the poor performance. And then there was the topic: big-game hunting in Africa. It was a topic few could relate to and took place on a continent even fewer could imagine ever visiting. Hemingway's virility shined even if the unadorned profanity did not. With regard to periodical contributions (articles, poems or short stories), Hemingway contributed to every monthly issue of *Esquire* (the most noteworthy "Notes on the Next War"). Additionally, he placed an article in the September issue of the *New Masses*.

1936

When he wasn't entertaining his regular flow of guests or looking for the thirteen-foot skiff he lost off Long Key (June 3), the author was writing with perfection. With regard to periodical contributions (articles, poems or short stories), Hemingway contributed six pieces to *Esquire*, the last of which was "The Snows of Kilimanjaro" (August). The major theme of the piece was death. Harry, a writer, and his wife, Helen, are stranded—thanks to their truck's broken engine—while on safari in Africa. As gangrene infects Harry's leg, it becomes clear that he is dying. Understanding this, Harry begins to reflect on his life. With brilliant construction, Hemingway narrates Harry's experiences in a stream of consciousness.

Hemingway also contributed one short story to *Cosmopolitan*, "The Short Happy Life of Francis Macomber" (September). Contrasting courage (character Robert Wilson) with fear (Francis Macomber), Hemingway constructed an impressive undercard (Francis Macomber versus Margot, his wife; Wilson versus Margot; Macomber versus his manhood; and much more), to borrow a boxing analogy. The author's literary prowess shined through his ambiguous, yet complex, characters and their conflicts.

Both "The Snows of Kilimanjaro" and "The Short Happy Life of Francis Macomber" solidified Ernest Hemingway as one of the finest short story writers of the twentieth century.[127]

1937

To Have and Have Not, set in Key West and Cuba, was published on October 15, 1937. Written sporadically between 1935 and 1937, two of the three Harry Morgan stories had previously appeared in periodicals.[128] Forever busy, Hemingway revised the work during his travels to and from Spain during the Spanish Civil War. The reception to the work was mixed.

Set during the Depression era, Harry Morgan, a fishing boat captain (a have not), turns to black-market activity owing to the economic conditions. The author contrasted the "haves" with the "have nots" by using a wealthy fishing charter customer to bilk Harry out of the expense of a three-week fishing trip. Harry also gets caught up in murder and smuggling. Intermingled with the story are chapters that describe the dissolute lives of wealthy yacht owners (haves).

A view of fishermen's boats docked at Key West in January 1938, almost like a scene out of the novel *To Have and Have Not*. *Library of Congress, LC-DIG-fsa-8a09356 (digital file from original neg.)*.

With regard to periodical contributions (articles, poems or short stories), Hemingway contributed his first report from Spain to the *New Republic*.

The Spanish Earth, an anti-fascist film directed by Joris Ivens, was released on July 11, 1937. Written by John Dos Passos and Ernest Hemingway, narrated by Orson Welles and re-recorded by Hemingway (with Jean Renoir doing the narration in the French release), with music composed by Marc Blitzstein and arranged by Virgil Thomson, it would be produced in book form in 1938.

1938

The Spanish Civil War, which began on July 17, 1936, had grown intense. Hemingway, stimulated by conflict, planned to be right in the thick of things. His first book release of the year, *The Spanish Earth*, published by J.B. Savage Company, was a transcript of the spoken commentary prepared by the author for the Loyalist film of the same title. The Loyalists, who supported the Second Spanish Republic, were fighting against the Nationalists (conservatives, Falangists, fascists, monarchists and traditionalists).[129] The Nationalists won the war, which ended in early 1939, and ruled Spain until Francisco Franco's death in November 1975.

The Fifth Column and the First Forty-Nine Stories was published by Scribner's on October 14, 1938. The book contains Hemingway's only full-length play, *The Fifth Column*, and forty-nine short stories. All but four—"The Short Happy Life of Francis Macomber," "The Snows of Kilimanjaro," "The Capital of the World" and "Old Man at the Bridge"—had appeared in other books by the author.

With regard to periodical contributions (articles, poems or short stories), Hemingway contributed two short stories to *Esquire*, contributed thirteen pieces to the short-lived illustrated magazine *Ken* (the magazine's editor was Arnold Gingrich), continued having his bulletins reprinted in the *New Republic* (and *Fact*) and published one piece with *Verve*.

1939

One Saturday night in January, Hemingway, who was heckled by a broker at the Stork Club in New York, sent him to dreamland with a solid left hand to the chin. His "tough guy" image preceded him everywhere he went. It was publicity he didn't need, but with no new book releases, it kept his name in print. (Most of the other ink he received that year detailed his fishing exploits.) With regard to periodical contributions (articles, poems or short stories), Hemingway contributed two short stories for *Cosmopolitan*, one (his last, "Night Before Battle") for *Esquire*, one (his last) for *Ken*, one (his last) for *New Masses* and one for *Vogue*.

1940

In June, Scribner's released a separate edition of *The Fifth Column* to coincide with the Broadway production of the play. The production drew accolades for its ability to capture the spirit of a courageous proletariat that stood up against an aggressive force (Hitler-Mussolini-Franco) for nearly three years. But on October 21, all eyes focused on Hemingway's latest release, *For Whom the Bell Tolls*.[130] Having labored on the book for seventeen months, the author was delighted at the results—it would be his most successful book. Ecstatic as well, Paramount Pictures purchased rights to the work for $100,000. For those who track such negotiations, that's twice the amount Margaret Mitchell put in her purse for *Gone with the Wind*.

Take a minute, and extract all the work from the résumé of Ernest Miller Hemingway. It is easy to conclude: his time in Key West produced quality work at an extraordinary level of productivity. Additionally, you have a clear picture of his talent as a writer, both before and after his time in Florida. There wasn't a work published after this time that didn't embrace something of relevance from this period of his life. It was time well spent.

7

FROM SOUVENIRS TO TREASURES

Ready to visit, or perhaps revisit, Ernest Hemingway's prolific body of work? Having walked in the footsteps of the literary giant, it is not a surprise. But what may amaze you is the vast amount of Hemingway artifacts. Acquiring and reading the author's books alone presents a challenge. And that's only the beginning. Other options, including books by some of his friends, associates and even members of his family, contribute to the intrigue. Regardless of what path you take, it is a great way to add to your Hemingway knowledge base.[131]

Books are only the tip of the iceberg when it comes to Hemingway souvenirs and treasures. There is a plethora of items available. But before you set sail toward a particular area, understand your parameters. Certain items, like first editions, letters penned by the author and even items he owned, can be challenging to find and expensive to purchase. And like any area of collectibles, they will require space and perhaps even preservation— let me also add patience, to complete the alliteration. For example, the John F. Kennedy Presidential Library houses an estimated 95 percent of the author's correspondence. Therefore, collecting his letters will limit you right from the start. But the challenge, not to mention the thrill, of owning a piece of "Papa" is hard to ignore.

Collectors split Hemingway collectibles into two distinct fields: items produced during his lifetime and posthumously produced products. Many simplify matters by picking a form to specialize in, such as magazines or film-related items. You will want to pick an area of collecting that won't limit your availability or finances yet allow you to have fun. If you do choose to specialize in a particular form, purchasing a resource dedicated to that area of collecting is recommended. Also, establish a budget for your avocation.

Take a brief glimpse—space does not allow for a comprehensive look at offerings available following the author's death—into the world of Ernest Hemingway.

ADVERTISING

As advertising comes in various forms, from pamphlets to postcards, even magazines or radio commercials, a collector has choices. A popular form is magazine advertising, such as the author's two-page spread for Ballantine Ale, the author's single-page pitch for the book *The Education of a French Model* or even a magazine or newspaper advertising one of his classic works put to film, such as *The Killers*. Unlike books, this material can be easier to find and far less expensive.

BOOKS

A number of good resources dedicated to collecting Hemingway's works on paper exist. *Ernest Hemingway, A Comprehensive Bibliography*, by Audre Hanneman, published by Princeton University Press in 1967, has always proved useful to collectors. Comprehensive, it covers books, pamphlets, newspapers and periodicals, translations, anthologies and much more.

First Editions

Collecting Hemingway first editions requires an education beyond the scope of this book. Take full advantage of what resources you can find. And don't be afraid to consult with a dealer or collector who specializes in this area. The first piece of information every Hemingway book collector learns: Regarding books published by Scribner's since 1930, first editions are indicated with a capital "A" on the copyright page.[132] The second fact: Rarity and condition, which includes the dust jacket, will determine value. For example, a copy of Hemingway's first book, *Three Stories & Ten Poems* (1923), from an initial print run of three hundred copies, sold for $81,250 at

COPYRIGHT, 1935, BY
CHARLES SCRIBNER'S SONS

Printed in the United States of America

All rights reserved. No part of this book may be reproduced in any form without the permission of Charles Scribner's Sons

A

The first piece of information every Hemingway book collector learns: On books published by Scribner's since 1930, first editions are indicated with a capital "A" on the copyright page. (Detail of copyright page.)

Written in 1951, *The Old Man and the Sea* is Ernest Hemingway's final full-length work published during his lifetime. The first-edition print run of the book was fifty thousand copies, and five million copies of *LIFE* magazine, where the book also appeared, were sold in two days.

a rare book auction held in 2012. The book published by Robert McAlmon at the Contact Publishing Company (Paris) has for years been a sought-after acquisition for serious book collectors. The original price was $2.00.

Naturally, not everyone can find or afford such an example. Alternatives include beginning your collection with later first editions or collecting subsequent printings. *For Whom the Bell Tolls* was published on October 21, 1940, at a purchase price of $2.75. It had an initial print run of 75,000 copies. That sounds like a lot of copies, which it was; however, the book sold nearly 200,000 copies by the end of the year. Fifty years later, finding an initial printing of the book, without a dust jacket, was achievable and inexpensive. This could be a good place to begin your first-edition book collecting.

Subsequent Editions

Subsequent releases of Hemingway titles can be confusing. Looking at *For Whom the Bell Tolls,* you have advance copies and salesman samples (both rare), a Book-of-the-Month Club (1940, 135,000 initial printing), a reprint edition published by P.F. Collier & Son Corporation (6-volume set), a limited illustrated edition published by Princeton University Press (1942, also 15 presentation copies), overseas edition published by Overseas Editions Inc., 4 reprint editions (1944, Grosset & Dunlap, Doubleday, Sun Dial Books, The Blakiston Company) and then you get to the first paperback edition (1951, Bantam Books). Even though a challenging area to collect, it can be fun and affordable. Also, many of the editions are beautifully presented.

Paperbacks

The colorful and illustrative covers of Hemingway paperbacks, indicative of the period, have always been enjoyable to collect. They are often interesting and inexpensive. For example, the first edition of *A Farewell to Arms* was published on September 27, 1929. The title was an enormous success and reprinted many times. Bantam Books published its paperback edition (No. 467) in January 1949. It featured an illustration of a romantic interlude done by popular commercial artist C.C. Beall (Cecil Calvert Beall). This edition was followed by reissue (1954) in Bantam larger format, called "A Bantam Giant" (A 1240) and priced at thirty-five cents. This edition featured an orange and blue illustration on the front cover, and a black-and-white photograph of Hemingway taken by A.E. Hotchner on the back. It was followed in 1955 by a black and yellow (two-color) version featuring a portrait of Hemingway, taken by A.E. Hotchner, on the front cover. The back cover featured a small drawing of Hemingway along with

The often colorful and illustrative covers of Hemingway paperbacks have always been enjoyable to collect. Indicative of the period, many are common and inexpensive.

a quote from Birger Ekeberg, president, Nobel Foundation. This version also sold for thirty-five cents. Later versions exist and offer an interesting alternative to hardcovers.

FILMS

Films, like books, are a specialized area of collecting. Serious collectors should pursue resources on the topic prior to making a major purchase. The release of a major film involved considerable publicity, along with associated marketing tools. Common forms of publicity: one-sheet posters (27" x 41"), half-sheet posters (22" x 28"), lobby cards (heavier stock, 11" x 14" and 14" x 17") and movie stills or photographs (8" x 10"). Later, larger three sheets (two pieces joined together, 41" x 80") were also used, as were other forms.

Here is a selected list of Hemingway on film: *A Farewell to Arms* (1932), *For Whom the Bell Tolls* (1943), *To Have and Have Not* (1944), *The Killers* (1946), *The Macomber Affair* (1947), *The Breaking Point* (1950), *Under My Skin* (1950), *The Snows of Kilimanjaro* (1952), *The Killers* (1956), *The Sun Also Rises* (1957), *A Farewell to Arms* (1957), *The Gun Runners* (1958), *The Old Man and the Sea*

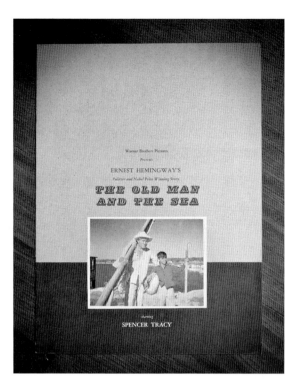

Right: Remember that there are items produced in conjunction with film premieres. They include press kits, photographs, invitations and even programs. Pictured is the Warner Brothers Pictures program for *The Old Man and the Sea*, starring Spencer Tracy.

Below: Pictured here is a 1950 Decca LP containing music from two soundtracks including *For Whom the Bell Tolls* (*FWTBT*, *left*), a later *FWTBT* soundtrack that featured Ingrid Bergman on the cover (*middle*) and the soundtrack for *Hemingway's Adventures of a Young Man* (*right*).

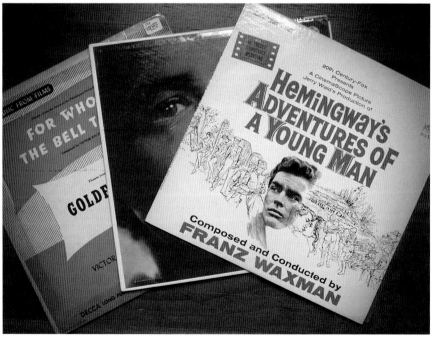

(1958) and later *Adventures of a Young Man* (1962), *The Killers* (1964), *Soldier's Home* (1977), *Islands in the Stream* (1977), *The Sun Also Rises* (1984), *The Old Man and the Sea* (1990), *The Old Man and the Sea* (1999), *After the Storm* (2001) and *Hemingway's Garden of Eden* (2008).[133]

Remember: Articles, photographs, reviews about the film and even souvenir programs can prove interesting. And don't overlook soundtracks.

LETTERS, NOTES AND AUTOGRAPHS

Not only can you walk in Hemingway's footsteps, but given the right circumstance you could also own something he held or even wrote. Even before the author's death in 1961, his written material was expensive. In the wake of his death, the demand exceeded availability. Ernest Hemingway was to literature what Babe Ruth was to baseball: an investment. Institutions, and prominent investors, scrambled to acquire items, as it was prestigious to have Hemingway material as part of a major collection or university archive. The author also became a must-have for every major autograph dealer and collector.

How much you will pay for a letter written by Ernest Hemingway will depend on whether it is handwritten or typed, its condition and—most of all—its content.[134] A Hemingway letter written about bullfighting, fishing and hunting will be worth far more than a routine correspondence. But be mindful that any letters are currently difficult to find in the market. Also, items dated prior to 1930 or before the release of *A Farewell to Arms* are scarce.

Ernest Hemingway, especially during the early years, wrote on whatever paper was available. Correspondence might even be written on a mix of stationery. When he ran out of space, he would use the margins. His handwriting was distinct and easy to authenticate for the experienced collector. As a prolific letter writer, Hemingway often signed his letters in a variety of ways. Some examples: E.H., Ernest, Ernie, E. Hemingway, Ernest Hemingway, Ernest M. Hemingway, Ernesto, Hem, Hemingway, Hemingstein, Hemmy, Mister Papa, Mr. Pappa, Papa (after 1926, frequent after 1940), Pappy, Steen, Stein, Taty or Tatey (to Hadley), Wemedge, Ye and numerous other one-off variations.

Hemingway's signature is classic and instantly recognizable. Collectors prefer a dark full name signature over other variations. However—and there is always a however in collecting—if the content is strong or the form unique, it could be a treasure. Whereas Hemingway was a prolific writer, he detested

Two rare Hemingway artifacts. Payment for Ernest Hemingway's first two articles for *Esquire* magazine (*top*); envelope addressed to Arnold Gingri(t)ch that contained Hemingway's article "A Spanish Letter." The envelope bears the printed address of the Piggott Land Company, which was owned by his father-in-law.

autograph collectors. Yes, he occasionally signed autographs, photographs, books and scraps of paper, but it often required prompting.

As he kept a small notepad with him at all times, Hemingway often recorded information by hand, be it addresses, phone numbers or even book ideas. Over the years, pages from his notepad have surfaced in the autograph market. While they are in the author's hand and some have interesting content, most do not have a signature.

Finally, a word or two about value. With regard to retail pricing, I would not sell a full Hemingway signature, in cut form, for under $2,000. (Other variations of his signature, I would. But not a full "Ernest Hemingway" signature.) Estimates regarding other forms are difficult, but don't be surprised to see an ordinary typed answer to an autograph request at retail price of $3,500 and a simple handwritten note at $4,500. A handwritten letter of significant content (bullfighting, fishing, hunting or even a reference to *The Old Man and the Sea*) can easily retail for three to four times the value of a typical note.[135]

Christmas Cards

Forgotten areas of collecting, like holiday cards, are not easy to come across but can be an interesting form to collect. If a collector does find Christmas cards in the market, they will likely be after 1945. Ernest married Mary Welsh in March 1946. The couple lived in Cuba for many years and, after 1959, in

If a collector does find Christmas cards in the market, they will likely be after 1945. Ernest married Mary Welsh in March 1946. The couple lived in Cuba for many years and, after 1959, in Ketchum, Idaho. This is the inside of two holidays cards signed by Mary Hemingway.

Ketchum, Idaho. Mary picked out the holiday cards, which were typical in design and message, and handled the bulk of the mailing. The cards could reflect their recent travels, which made them even more interesting. Many of the Cuban Christmas cards feature island designs and Spanish messages. And in some instances, "Ernest and Mary Hemingway" was printed inside the card. (The couple could add a short-handwritten note. Ernest would often sign "Ernie" and Mary only an "M.") A favorite of many collectors are those cards that originated from Africa. On occasion, Mary would buy cards from the East African Wild Life Society (correct spelling) that were spectacular in design. Depending on Ernest's mood, he could write a short note inside a card or a long note. (Examples ranging from 1 word to over 150 words have entered the market. Typical of his writing, if space was limited on the card, he would write in the margins.) On rare occasions, Mary shared personal information. For example, I was surprised to find her sharing details in one holiday card about the couple's visit to the Mayo Clinic.

ERNEST HEMINGWAY'S FILE—FEDERAL BUREAU OF INVESTIGATION

Of all the interesting Hemingway documents that have entered the market over the years, this form generates the most curiosity. Through the Freedom of Information Act, collectors can apply for the FBI's file on Ernest Hemingway. For example, when this author applied for a copy, I received

125 pages of documents at no charge (thanks to another requester, or I would have had a charge for the service) with a copy of the explanation of the exemptions.[136] It is a fascinating read, despite the redactions, for anyone interested in the author.

"Consequently, early in September 1942, ERNEST HEMINGWAY began to engage directly in intelligence activities in behalf of the American Embassy in Havana," said a legal attaché to Director J. Edgar Hoover.[137] This is one of many intriguing lines that fill the file. Looking at a few others: "At the present time he is alleged to be performing a highly secret naval operation for the Navy Department. In this connection, the Navy Department is said to be paying the expenses for the operation of Hemingway's boat, furnishing him with arms and charting courses in the Cuban area";[138] "Concerning the picture *For Whom the Bell Tolls*, Hemingway stated that he has no desire to see it because he does not believe it is a true portrayal of his work.… Furthermore, Gary Cooper is past his prime and he does not consider his choice as a leading man a happy one";[139] and a Havana letter dated August 26, 1954, furnished the details of a disagreement between novelist Ernest Hemingway and columnist Edward "Ted" Scott, as a result of which Scott challenged Hemingway to a duel. (Hemingway had no intention of dueling with Scott because of ill health and his work. Unsatisfied with Hemingway's answer, Scott did not know what else to do about this matter.)[140] As expected, all Hemingway's political ties are noted. The file does mention his visits to Mayo Clinic in Rochester, Minnesota.

Magazines

No stranger to the magazine world, Ernest Hemingway appeared in many of the most popular periodicals of the era. Articles by or about the author can be found in: *Argosy*, *The Atlantic Monthly*, *Avon*, *Bachelor*, *Climax*, *Collier's*, *Cosmopolitan*, *Esquire*, *Fortune*, *Golden Book Magazine*, *Holiday*, *Ken*, *Life*, *Jack London's Adventure*, *Look*, *Man's*, *Nash's Pall Mall*, *Poetry*, *The New Republic*, *The New Yorker*, *Reader's Digest*, *Scribner's*, *The Saturday Evening Post*, *Sports Illustrated*, *Time*, *True*, *Victory* and *Wisdom*, to name most.

Magazine collectors favor key issues, such as the first by *Esquire* (Volume 1, No. 1), prepublication serial appearances of the author's novel or *Cosmopolitan*'s five-part publication of *Across the River and into the Trees* and magazines that feature Hemingway prominently on the cover. Issues such as the September 1, 1952 *Life* magazine that not only feature the author on the cover but also the first publication of his new book, *The Old Man and the Sea*, remain prized by collectors despite it being a mass-produced publication.

Like all collectibles, condition is a critical factor when determining value. Newsstand issues that do not have a mailing label are favored over subscription copies. If a magazine has a subscriber label attached and it detracts from the cover, it will reduce the value. Content, such as work by other popular writers and illustrators, will affect value. If you are purchasing items via mail, be forewarned: magazines like early issues of *Esquire* will weigh more than anticipated.

Pamphlets and Brochures

An overlooked area of collecting is pamphlets, brochures and broadsides. Even if many are free and mass produced, they generally don't have a long shelf life. And as years pass, some have shown significant appreciation in price. For example, some Key West tourist brochures from the 1950s and 1960 have been routinely offered on auction internet sites for ten to twelve dollars.

Philatelic—Stamps and Cachets

Stamps, like books, have always been a specialized area of collecting. Therefore, you may want to review some dedicated resources before making any serious purchases. Ernest Hemingway has appeared on stamps produced in Australia, Cuba, Sweden and the United States. The most popular is likely the twenty-five-cent Literary Arts Series commemorative stamp (US #2418) that honored the author and was issued on July 17, 1989. The stamp dedication was held in two places: Key West and his birthplace of Oak Park, Illinois (souvenir programs exist for both locations). The designer of the stamp, which was the seventh in the Literary Arts Series, was M. Gregory Rudd of Trumbull, Connecticut. The stamp, once placed on a wide variety of first day covers (envelopes) or souvenir pages, makes the perfect display.

Postcards

It surprises some to learn that deltiology (the term for collecting postcards), is the third-largest hobby after collecting stamps and coins. The reason for it is availability, cost and enjoyment. Because the hobby is vast in scale, many collectors specialize in certain areas or eras.

Since Ernest Hemingway was an international celebrity, collectors will have plenty of collecting options—as if collecting postcards related to his life in Key West won't be enough to keep you busy. As the Hemingway House has been featured on many postcards over the years, it may be the perfect place to begin your collection.

It can be difficult to date postcards, but certain factors can help. When Ernest and Pauline arrived in Key West, white-bordered postcards were popular (until about 1930). That era was followed by the popular linen (paper with cotton fiber) postcards (1930–50). These cards were used to improve the brightness of the ink. A majority of many early postcards were printed by a process known as lithography, or images constructed using small dots. Prior to this process, "real photo" postcards were popular, or images constructed using the photography process, or continuous tones (no dots). "Real photo" postcards often command values five to ten times greater than lithograph postcards. Age, artist (if applicable), condition, composition and manufacturer are all important factors in determining value. Used postcards will have additional factors such as author, content, stamp and postmark.

Hemingway, who was partial to writing letters, seldom sent postcards. While they can contain interesting content, they seldom enter the market. Examples of those he sent to Gertrude Stein or even some on which he shared writing space with his fourth wife, Mary Welsh, can be viewed on certain internet sites.

Posters

Many collectors are surprised at how many posters of Ernest Hemingway exist. This was likely because there was little control over the production of images. Many bootleg posters exist and provide little, if any, information regarding the source. Serious collectors turn to posters of images taken by popular photographers such as Alfred Eisenstaedt or Yousuf Karsh.

Hemingway collectors associate Alfred Eisenstaedt (1898–1995) with his work for LIFE magazine. Not a surprise considering the magazine featured more than 90 of his pictures on its covers, and more than 2,500 of his photo stories. The most popular image, or poster, with collectors is his portrait of the author that appeared on the September 1, 1952 issue of LIFE magazine.

The most recognized portrait, or poster, of Ernest Hemingway—used as a reference for the stamp issued in the author's honor by the U.S. Postal Service—was taken by Yousuf Karsh (1908–2002). Karsh has been described as one of the greatest portrait photographers of the twentieth century, and his portrait of Hemingway—not to mention other iconic images such as a 1941 photograph of Winston Churchill—support the claim.[141]

Recordings

Audio recordings come in many formats; choose the one that best fits your requirements. From movie soundtracks to even Ernest Hemingway reading his own material, audio recordings are an interesting and cost-friendly area of collectibles. *Ernest Hemingway Reading* produced by Caedmon (TC–1185) is a must-have for any collection. The long-playing 33 1/-3rpm microgroove recording comprises the Nobel Prize Acceptance Speech, Second Poem to Mary, In Harry's Bar in Venice, *The Fifth Column*, Work in Progress and Saturday Night at the Whorehouse in Billings, Montana.

Souvenirs—Key West Related

Three great places to begin your Ernest Hemingway souvenir collecting are Captain Tony's Saloon, the Ernest Hemingway Home & Museum and Sloppy Joe's.

Captain Tony's Saloon, at 428 Greene Street, offers an interesting array of clothing, including: T-shirts (acid wash tees, basic T-shirts), long-sleeve shirts, classic v-neck shirts, hoodie sweatshirts, tank tops; hats and visors; koozies and coolies (can and bottle); magnets; signs; and stickers. And pick up a copy of Captain Tony Tarracino and Brad Manard's book *Life Lessons of a Legend*.

The Ernest Hemingway Home & Museum, located at 907 Whitehead Street, offers a wonderful selection of collectibles, including: virtual/digital media, apparel, gifts and souvenirs, home and décor, stationery, Hemingway's work and Tripp Harrison artwork. Favorite items: Picasso cat replica, paper weight, title white bookmark, billfish T-shirt, Hemingway journal, museum coin, stamp mug, Hemingway Writes T-shirt and mini museum book. Many collectors are partial to limited-edition items, dateable products and those products that feature the image of Ernest Hemingway. Any product that has a Hemingway House sticker or stamp is preferred over items that do not. All collectible products should be left in their original packaging. Do not remove anything related to the sale of the item, and save your admission ticket and even the bag that you used to carry your purchase.

Sloppy Joe's, at 201 Duval Street, offers an extensive line of clothing, glassware, party supplies and souvenirs. It even has an "On Sale" section on its website. Of the many items being offered, collectors seem to enjoy the products with the "classic logo" that features an image of Hemingway or limited-edition offerings. But do not overlook any unusual souvenirs, because they tend to have a short shelf life if they do not sell. Once again, and worth repeating: All collectible products should be left in original packaging. Do not remove anything related to the sale of the item and even save the bag that you used to carry your purchase. If you are at the bar, save your coaster, napkin and even a pack of matches.

8

THE HEMINGWAY MYTHOS

Take a minute, and compare the meaning of life—something we all share but perceive differently—to climbing a mountain. Knowing that the answer to that meaning rests at the summit, that mountaintop becomes your goal. Applying your skill to the ascent, along with your experience, brings you one step closer to the objective. Affected by the gradient, the complexity of the task increases as you progress. Each step is a question of your ability and a challenge to your senses. Understanding that the greater the risk the greater the reward motivates you to continue. Reaching the pinnacle challenges every aspect of your being. The greatest test is that of your courage. It is the breadth of that valor that determines your success. Only a few of us will reach the apex, but not many will have the capacity to look down. Yet that was the view Hemingway always desired. Edges meant nothing to the man.

There was Hemingway the writer and Hemingway the man, both equally fascinating. Both equally complex. Together, the combination created an unparalleled life.

HEMINGWAY THE WRITER

Challenge the reader, Ernest Hemingway believed. Show them what it is like to be human—how we live, love and relate to one another. Then force them to take a stand. Using the tools that you have given the reader, let them take

Right: There was Hemingway the writer and Hemingway the man, both equally fascinating. Both equally complex. Ernest Hemingway's 1923 passport (*detail*). *Ernest Hemingway Collection. John F. Kennedy Presidential Library and Museum, Boston.*

Below: Personal experience, or Ernest Hemingway's reserve fuel tank, was critical to his writing. Ernest Hemingway sitting by the pool at Finca Vigía, San Francisco de Paula, Cuba. *Ernest Hemingway Collection. John F. Kennedy Presidential Library and Museum, Boston.*

a position. What decision would they make? Digesting his work, we could picture the smirk on Hemingway's face. He took us out of our comfort zone, leaving us to choose between what we believed was moral or immoral. But regardless of our choice, we were seduced by the material presented and the complexity that surrounded it.

Personal experience, or Ernest Hemingway's reserve fuel tank, was critical to his writing. It was the security blanket he required for maximum production. As he wrote about his observations, it was difficult to separate fact from fiction—the latter nothing more than sustenance for "super liars," as he called writers of this genre. Part of him, and we could sense it, was incorporated in each work. Therefore, visiting his themes painted a self-portrait. They became his brush strokes. Common subjects in Hemingway prose are ambivalence, death, disillusionment, love and war, masculinity and nature.

Mixed feelings or contradictory ideas could be found in the heart of Nick Adams, Hemingway's autobiographical persona, and even in the heart of Liz Coates in the classic "Up in Michigan." The author understood that there was good along with bad in everyone, even himself.

Death seemed to always be at the tip of the author's fingers, be it as accidents, suicides or a result of war. The theme was so prevalent that *A Farewell to Arms* begins and ends with it. The inevitability of death bothered Hemingway. He challenged it and sought control over it. Yet in the end, he surrendered to it, when he took that control.

Discovering that life was not as good as one had hoped, or disillusionment, was an argument that lent itself to stories like "A Clean, Well-Lighted Place" and "The Capital of the World." The author enjoyed contrasting a tragic death against a life that had fallen short of expectation. Heroic fatalism, perhaps best handled in "The Killers," lent itself to this theme. Hemingway's protagonists are forced to—please excuse the idiom—play the hand they are dealt, as they say. And it was a circumstance he enjoyed writing about.

A Farewell to Arms and *For Whom the Bell Tolls* contrast love and war while presenting additional underpinnings, such as political ideology and even contemplating one's own death. In the latter, for example, death presents itself in nearly every scene—no need to knock, the readers understand it was always there. In typical Hemingway fashion, fate enters the picture as an ironic coincidence. While irony can be comical, frustrating or even tragic, it is part of life and something people can relate to.

Machismo, and the exaggeration of it, was to Hemingway like a home run was to Babe Ruth. It was a statement of courage, confidence and security.

Hemingway had the written word as a conduit for his feelings and fears. Ernest Hemingway sitting near a stream and writing, near San Ildefonso, Spain (1959). *Ernest Hemingway Collection. John F. Kennedy Presidential Library and Museum, Boston.*

That type of character, the author felt, was best displayed by a sportsman. A "real man" was a hunter capable of standing his ground in order to put a bullet between the eyes of a charging lion, or a fisherman willing to reel in a marlin after a two-hour struggle or any man willing to face fate without remorse. As a man's man, Hemingway understood the subject resonated with both men and women.

God's handiwork was a popular topic with the author. This is not a surprise considering he was a lifelong outdoorsman. After all, value in the form of hope and inspiration could be found in nature, such as a mountain or even a river. Hemingway even embraced keys, in the form of dreaming, hunting or fishing, to unlock that value.

Other themes, and there were many, were antisemitism, camaraderie, divination, early love, family disappointment, love, marital problems, political ideology and women, to name a few.

These themes worked for a number of reasons, not the least of which was timing. They struck a chord with a worldwide audience and confirmed Ernest Hemingway's status as the greatest American writer since Mark Twain. *The Old Man and the Sea* earned him a Pulitzer Prize in 1953 and the Nobel Prize for Literature in 1954. He mastered the art of narration thanks to one true sentence.

His productivity was also impressive. Hemingway seemed to have an endless supply of ideas that he transformed into successful standalone novels, short story collections or nonfiction books.

In Key West, a productive morning of writing in his studio inspired him to make the most of the afternoon aboard his boat. And a productive afternoon on the water led to an inventive evening on land. It wasn't only the cycle that was impressive but his ability to repeat it time after time.

Hemingway the Man

As the apotheosis of masculinity, Ernest Hemingway understood that fear was the only deterrent between him and what he sought. Since he possessed the solution, which was courage, he could quell any trepidation. He fought for what he believed in and enjoyed it. Adversity, he believed, would serve only to make him stronger—a pertinent yet overused expression. The strength of the author's courage was drawn from a positive and disciplined approach to his fears. Educating himself about the aversion conquered his phobias.

The written word was a conduit for his feelings and fears (If, of course, he had any aversions. Hey, it's Hemingway). As such an outlet, he was less vulnerable to criticism.[142] It was a safe.

When Ernest Hemingway did step out of his comfort zone, he seldom did it without preparation. People forget this about the man. For example, look at the capabilities of the Hemingway Mob and how much the author learned or benefited from them before he purchased his own boat. It would have been dangerous for the author, as a rookie sea captain, to navigate the shoals of the blue water surrounding Key West. And he knew it. On both his African safaris, the first taking place in 1934, Philip Percival, arguably the greatest hunter of his era, was Hemingway's guide. There was value associated with learning a skill from the very best.

After the release of *A Farewell to Arms* (1929), his sense of self-esteem or self-importance grew. And by *For Whom the Bell Tolls* (1940), his egomania lacked restraint. Feeding a caricature of yourself, as the author would learn, would not be uncomplicated.

Opinions change; classic works of literature do not. Ernest Hemingway seated aboard the *Pilar*. *Ernest Hemingway Collection. John F. Kennedy Presidential Library and Museum, Boston.*

THE HEMINGWAY MYTHOS

Unbridled masculine bravado, bolstered by extraordinary talent at peak efficiency, yet counterbalanced against gratification.

That's the Hemingway mythos, as many see it, even if it was a custom and complicated interpretation. Lost time, as both Benjamin Franklin and Ernest Hemingway understood, was never found again.

Ernest Hemingway was a son, novelist, brother, short-story writer, father, journalist, husband, hunter, lover, fisherman, friend, hunter, soldier, sailor, sea captain, boxer, bullfighter, you get the picture. As a man's man, he fit the bill. Every generation has its public he-man, and Ernest Hemingway, not unlike Douglas Fairbanks and Jack Dempsey, filled the literary seat at the table. While displays of his exaggerated manhood may have come and gone—Lord knows there were many, like the glossy photographs of him hunting kudu in Africa or fishing for billfish in the Straits of Florida—virility remains.

Hemingway's stimulus-driven Key West years were balanced (Hemingway the Man) with productivity (Hemingway the Writer). It was the Hemingway mythos, and it set the bar for many men. But before you load the gun and aim it at me, hear me out.

More than one person, over the past three generations, has wondered if they lived up to the Hemingway standard of manliness. And while more than one person has felt uncomfortable trying, more than one person has expressed little concern. Times have changed, and the author's positions on topics, such as women or hunting, for example, are considered flawed and no longer acceptable.

But—and there was always that annoying conjunction with regard to the author—one thing stands true: While opinions change, classic works of literature do not. For example, *The Sun Also Rises* still inspires its fair share of men (over one million visitors every year) to join the running of the bulls at Pamplona's Fiesta de San Fermín. And every year since—let me remind you the publication of the work was almost a century ago— the first name out of every person's mouth who attends the festival is Ernest Hemingway.

STREET REFERENCE
AND DISTANCES

This is an alphabetical street reference by route.

Route One, Fifteen Locations

Emma Street
Fitzpatrick Street
Front Street
Howard England Way
Petronia Street
South Street
Thomas Street
United Street
Wall Street
Whitehead Street

Route Two, Forty-Seven Locations

Angela Street
Ashe Street
Caroline Street
Duval Street
Eaton Street

Fleming Street
Greene Street
Grinnell Street
Margaret Street
Passover Lane
Reynolds Street
Simonton Street
South Street
Southard Street
Varela Street
Windsor Lane

ROUTE THREE, TEN LOCATIONS

Atlantic Boulevard
Duncan Street
Olivia Street
Pearl Street
Pine Street
Roosevelt Boulevard
Seminary Street

CROSS REFERENCE—STREET/ROUTE

This is an alphabetical master cross-reference. If a Key West street is not on this list, then it is not part of the suggested routes.

Angela Street (Route 2)
Ashe Street (Route 2)
Atlantic Boulevard (Route 3)
Caroline Street (Route 2)
Duncan Street (Route 3)
Duval Street (Route 2)
Eaton Street (Route 2)
Emma Street (Route 1)
Fitzpatrick Street (Route 1)
Fleming Street (Route 2)

Front Street (Route 1)
Greene Street (Route 2)
Grinnell Street (Route 2)
Howard England Way (Route 1)
Margaret Street (Route 2)
Olivia Street (Route 3)
Passover Lane (Route 2)
Pearl Street (Route 3)
Pine Street (Route 3)
Petronia Street (Route 1)
Reynolds Street (Route 2)
Roosevelt Boulevard (Route 3)
Seminary Street (Route 3)
Simonton Street (Route 2)
South Street (Route 1, Route 2)
Southard Street (Route 2)
Thomas Street (Route 1)
United Street (Route 1)
Varela Street (Route 2)
Wall Street (Route 1)
Whitehead Street (Route 1)
Windsor Lane (Route 2)

DISTANCE REFERENCE—SELECTED LOCATIONS

From	To	Distance*	Walking	Automobile
Key West Express	Sloppy Joe's	0.5 miles	12 minutes	7 minutes
Key West Express	Crowne Plaza/ La Concha	0.9 miles	15 minutes	7 minutes
Key West Express	Margaritaville	0.7 miles	16 minutes	6 minutes
Key West Express	Ernest Hemingway House	1.2 miles	24 minutes	8 minutes
Key West Express	Casa Marina Resort	1.5 miles	31 minutes	11 minutes

From	To	Distance*	Walking	Automobile
Key West Int. Airport	Casa Marina Resort	4.0 miles	53 minutes	12 minutes
Key West Int. Airport	Sloppy Joe's	5.3 miles	85 minutes	19 minutes
Mallory Square	Sloppy Joe's	0.2 miles	4 minutes	4 minutes
Mallory Square	Margaritaville	0.5 miles	10 minutes	6 minutes
Mallory Square	Ernest Hemingway House	0.9 miles	16 minutes	9 minutes
Mallory Square	Lighthouse & Keeper's…	0.9 miles	17 minutes	9 minutes
Mallory Square	Key West Cemetery	1.0 miles	22 minutes	10 minutes
Mallory Square	Southernmost Point	1.3 miles	24 minutes	11 minutes
Mallory Square	Casa Marina Resort	1.7 miles	38 minutes	14 minutes
Mallory Square	Key West Int. Airport	4.3 miles	88 minutes	20 minutes
Margaritaville	Southernmost Point	0.8 miles	18 minutes	7 minutes
Sloppy Joe's	Ernest Hemingway House	0.7 miles	15 minutes	6 minutes
Sloppy Joe's	Casa Marina Resort	1.5 miles	34 minutes	11 minutes
Thompson Docks	Ernest Hemingway House	1.0 miles	22 minutes	8 minutes

(208 Margaret St.)

*Distance by car, which can be longer than walking.

NOTES

Introduction

1. Hemingway's fascination with bullfighting originated from his love of boxing. The author compared the bull's use of his horns to that of a pugilist throwing a combination.
2. The name of the author's article was "A Matter of Colour."
3. The article, so some critics believed, revealed Hemingway's racism. According to his Black sparring partners, the author was not a racist.
4. Harold Loeb had a brief affair with British socialite Duff "Lady" Twysden. Hemingway later used them as inspiration for the characters of Robert Cohn and Lady Brett Ashley in his roman à clef *The Sun Also Rises*—Loeb was often recognized as the initial target for Hemingway's backhanded opprobrium.
5. Critics viewed Cohn not as a sportsman but an athlete; he used boxing to shroud his Jewishness.
6. Hemingway's boxing narrative exhibits knowledge and precision, with a good understanding of the value of techniques such as feints and head movement.
7. It was proof that the author was never far from reality.
8. The piece would also appear in other short story collections.
9. Andre Anderson, whose real name was Frederick Boeseneilers, died on April 1, 1926.

10. The author details aspects of this relationship in his book *The World Colored Heavyweight Championship, 1876–1937 (Drawing the Color Line)* published by McFarland Company Inc., 2020.
11. Robert Cohn, in *The Sun Also Rises*, has a boxing background.
12. There were occasions when Hemingway paid his sparring partners a flat rate of two dollars.
13. Iron Baby Roberts even made a trip to Cuba with the author aboard the *Pilar*.

1. Ernest Hemingway's Key West (1928–1940)

14. Legendary editor Thomas W. Johnston Jr. was the man behind the literary tool.
15. Elizabeth Hadley Richardson was born on November 9, 1891, in St. Louis, Missouri. She was the youngest of five children.
16. Hemingway wanted *The Sun Also Rises* to be published by Scribner's. In December 1925, he expediently penned *The Torrents of Spring*—a satirical work attacking Boni & Liveright's meal ticket Sherwood Anderson—in order to terminate his contract. His three-book contract with the firm included a termination clause should they reject a single submission. They rejected Hemingway's submission. Weeks later, Scribner's agreed to publish *The Torrents of Spring* and all of his subsequent work.
17. This record high temperature was matched on August 26, 1956.
18. This accomplishment courtesy of Henry M. Flagler.
19. Vessels carrying thirty feet of water anchored in the outer harbor, while those carrying twenty-six feet could dock in the inner harbor.
20. At its peak, the company operated seventy ships.
21. U.S. Decennial Census.
22. Gus Pfeiffer made his fortune as a commodity broker. Later, his land investments proved fruitful.
23. The shipment of their automobile, from Miami, had been delayed a week; their apartment was in the rear of the building on the second floor.
24. See Hemingway, Ernest M., EH to Maxwell Perkins, April 21, 1928, Letter, Princeton University Library, Princeton, New Jersey.
25. "Georgie" Brooks was the state prosecuting attorney for the Keys.
26. Hemingway, wanting to know about everything he was experiencing, interrogated Saunders like he was on trial. He even questioned the

experienced mariner about the best way to prepare snapper and yellowtail for cooking.

27. The integration of his friendship base was a common trait with Hemingway. He would eventually integrate his Key West Mob with that of his Sun Valley group.

28. Some sources claim Delmonico's; however, it was called Delmonico Restaurant.

29. The Florida record is over 240 pounds; the event was captured for posterity on camera by Bill Smith, who witnessed Peirce even wrestling with the fish during the final moments.

30. Not every resource would claim Edward "Bra(w)" Saunders as a secondary source for the character.

31. Pauline's father came to Key West in May and drove back to Piggott with Ernest in the new Model A Ford.

32. On November 17, Ernest and Pauline stayed overnight at the home of F. Scott and Zelda Fitzgerald. They had attended a football game between Princeton and Yale at Palmer Stadium. After hearing of the death of his father, Ernest wired Fitzgerald for a loan.

33. Strater was unavailable, so Fitzgerald wired Hemingway the money.

34. Serialization for the book, in *Scribner's Magazine*, garnered Hemingway $10,000—some sources claim $16,000. This took place prior to book publication.

35. In 1926, while in Paris, Hemingway purchased *The Farm* by the artist.

36. There were also many other journeys in and around the island of Key West. Even Pauline and Lorine Thompson managed to land some good-size tarpon.

37. Pauline's uncle Gustavus Adolphus Pfeiffer underwrote the African safari to a tune of $25,000; both projects supported Hemingway's belief that it was an individual's approach toward death that was more important than death itself. And both projects were a natural progression from the "grace under pressure" work of *A Farewell To Arms*.

38. Ernest stayed at a dude ranch located twelve miles from Cooke City, Montana. It was owned by Lawrence and Olive Nordquist.

39. Ernest's arm was set at least three times and operated on once.

40. The Hemingway clan hoped to leave Piggott, Arkansas, by January 3, 1932.

41. Chub Weaver had driven the Ford from Montana to Arkansas to Florida and was living in a Key West boardinghouse; the Mob also hosted Pat and Maude Morgan.

42. The trip out to the Tortugas lasted thirteen days. Chub Weaver, from Montana, was on vacation.

43. Russell's watercraft was named after his daughter Anita Russell Cates (1917–1952). Russell charged Hemingway ten dollars a day charter fee for the *Anita*.

44. The trip to the Dry Tortugas lasted eighteen days. Ernest's taste for marlin fishing seemed to grow with each passing excursion.

45. According to sources, this was when his relationship with Jane Mason began.

46. Russell, acting as tour guide, handled excursion, hotel and shuttling expenses; Jane Mason and her husband, Grant, lived west of Havana. She even joined the group aboard the *Anita* for an excursion in May.

47. The children came down with whooping cough (pertussis), which is highly contagious and affects the lungs. Ernest stayed behind to finish up the house renovations.

48. Ernest and Pauline lost nearly all their clothing and some personal belongings (including some firearms) in a fire at the studio they occupied at the home of Paul M. Pfeiffer on December 15, 1932.

49. Moving from quarterly to monthly, *Esquire* published twenty-five articles and six short stories by Hemingway (1933–1939).

50. The frequency of Hemingway family travel surprises many, especially considering the times.

51. Marlene Dietrich and Katharine Hepburn, who were on the same ship as Ernest and Pauline Hemingway, garnered most of the headlines upon the ship's arrival.

52. Arnold Gingrich was aware of Hemingway's desire to purchase his own boat. By advancing the author $3,000 against future *Esquire* articles, Gingrich could secure Hemingway's participation. And the editor believed Hemingway's new toy would inspire the writer; the *Pilar* cost the author $7,495.

53. Hemingway dressed in casual clothes—he always wore shorts with a rope for a belt and Indian moccasins.

54. On their way to the coast of Venezuela, Leicester Hemingway and Al Dudek stopped over in Key West.

55. Without question Hemingway was also interested in having the group underwrite some, if not all, of the costs associated with the trip. Pauline and Patrick left for Arkansas on May 30, 1934; Pauline planned to meet up with Ernest on July 19 in Havana. Sidney Franklin, famous American-Spanish matador, also planned to join Ernest in Havana. The pair hoped to enjoy several days of fishing.

56. Emersed in his Key West lifestyle, Ernest was none too happy about the drive to Piggott; Arnold Gingrich and John Dos Passos joined Hemingway for a brief fishing excursion during the first week of December.

57. Hemingway had hoped that the work would draw an offer for at least $10,000, which it did for *Cosmopolitan* if Hemingway reduced the word count. In the end, Max Perkins took the piece for $5,000.

58. The trip back to Key West from Bimini took twenty-six hours. This was the most intense Atlantic hurricane to make landfall in terms of pressure (892 millibars). The storm packed a recorded wind gust of 185 miles per hour; nothing in its path was safe.

59. Conrad Van Hyning, Florida ERA administrator, who happened to be staying at the commandant's quarters at the naval station, joined Ernest on a fishing trip at the end of December—the excursion a quid pro quo for the *Pilar*'s use of the submarine pen.

60. Other guests included Burris Jenkins (cartoonist), Bill Cleveland (aviator), J.A. Conable, Richard Cooper, Cecil Gray (taxidermist), Heble Todd (immigration service) and Seward Webb, to name a few.

61. Pauline would join the group in Havana on May 12. She, along with her son Gregory, had recently arrived back from Piggott.

62. Bimini comprises a chain of islands located a mere fifty miles due east of Miami—the closest point of the Bahamas to the mainland. The waters that surround the islands are a haven for marlin, tuna and swordfish. If Hemingway docked and spent the night, it was often at the Compleat Angler Hotel (1935). Located in the center of Alice Town, it contained twelve guestrooms and a popular bar. It was destroyed by a fire in 2006.

63. The original titles of these works were, respectively: "The Happy Ending" and "A Budding Friendship."

64. The fifty-two-minute film, narrated by Orson Welles (English), Ernest Hemingway (English) and Jean Renoir (French), was released on July 11, 1937.

65. Hemingway, bound for Miami, left by plane on January 10, 1937. The pair left on the same northbound train from Miami, but Ernest departed en route.

66. Sidney Franklin, Brooklyn matador, was also on the same boat; supporters of the Spanish Republic—John Dos Passos, Ernest Hemingway and Orson Welles—intended to raise money for the Republican cause by working on a film, Joris Ivens's documentary *The Spanish Earth*.

67. Hemingway boarded the *Pilar* and set sail on May 26, 1937. While in Cat Cay, Bahamas, Ernest took a few trips to New York City, the West Coast and Washington, D.C.

68. The day before sailing for Spain, Hemingway, a heavyweight, tangled with Max Eastman, a light heavyweight, in the office of editor Maxwell Perkins of Charles Scribner's Sons. "He-man" Hemingway, after displaying his chest hair, threw Eastman's book, *Bull in the Afternoon*, at the author. Accounts of the action varied from this point forward.

69. *The Fifth Column* was Hemingway's only full-length play. It was released, along with forty-nine short stories, in book form on October 14, 1938. Published by Scribner's, the work included four recent stories (1936), one old story (1923), sixteen stories from *In Our Time* (1925), fourteen stories from *Men Without Women*, and fourteen stories from *Winner Take Nothing* (1933).

70. They returned from France aboard *Gripsholm* on January 12, 1938; Ernest and Pauline sailed to Miami, picked up the *Pilar* and then headed off to Key West. It was not a comfortable trip. They arrived home after that month.

71. Pauline joined Ernest on the flight to Miami. Ernest then entrained for New York before taking passage to Spain. Pauline, after a brief stay, returned to Key West.

72. On May 31, Hemingway arrived in New York aboard the *Normandie*.

73. On June 22, 1938, Hemingway flew to New York City to attend the *Joe Louis v. Max Schmeling* rematch.

74. During the first week of July, the Overseas Highway was formally opened to the motoring public.

75. Rather than being pinned down in Key West, Ernest would head to Spain and ask Toby Bruce to chauffer the family to and from Piggott. Ernest sailed for Europe on August 31.

76. Pauline had rented an apartment on East 50th Street in New York City.

77. Naturally, it didn't take long for Ernest to establish his Sun Valley Mob. Unlike the early days of his Key West associations, Hemingway was now a celebrity. Finding associates, or hangers-on if you will, would not be an issue.

78. Hemingway was joined by some guests, including J.S. Kelly, owner of the Brooklyn Dodgers.

79. See "Hemingway Here; Going to China," *Key West Citizen*, December 21, 1940. Hemingway, along with Patrick and Gregory, departed Key West aboard the SS *Cuba*, bound for Havana, on December 23, 1940. Author Sinclair Lewis was also aboard the ship. Staying in Key West, Pauline went into business with Lorine Thompson. The pair owned the Caroline Decorating Shop on Caroline Street.

80. Ernest Hemingway was divorced from his second wife, Pauline Pfeiffer Hemingway, on November 4, 1940. Pauline received the Key West home on Whitehead Street and custody of the couple's two sons. Neither principals were present as the suit was heard by Judge Arthur Gomez; Ernest Hemingway's final trip to Key West took place in late July 1960. Ernest, along with his last wife, Mary, stayed at the Santa Maria Motel at 1401 Simonton Street.

2. Hemingway's Mob, Associates and Assorted Guests

81. There was an art to choreographing execution, and Hemingway proved it; he also proved that fiction describes imaginary events and people that weren't so hard to imagine.
82. A commonality was the passion for their profession and, in some cases, unquestioned expertise in their craft.
83. Not to mention the chance of a fisherman like Albert Pinder meeting a poet like Archibald MacLeish was improbable.
84. Reynolds admired Hemingway's work and could articulately speak about the sport of boxing.
85. Hemingway and Dos Passos had a falling out over José Robles, a left-wing aristocrat who was arrested and shot as a Fascist spy. Robles was going to assist both writers on their film project.
86. John Dos Passos married Mary Elizabeth Hamlin (1909–1998) in 1949.
87. In 1942, the Hickoks were living in New Canaan, Connecticut.
88. The affair was believed to have lasted from 1932 until 1936; Mason became the inspiration behind Margot Macomber in the Hemingway short story "The Short Happy Life of Francis Macomber."
89. James H. Pinder died at the family home at 815 Fleming Street in 1939.
90. Julia Saunders's birth year varies by source. Her grave marker indicates 1874.
91. As fate might have it, not far from where this author's uncle is buried.
92. See EH to Maxwell Perkins, April 21, 1928, at Princeton University Library, Princeton, New Jersey; also in Carlos Baker, ed., *Ernest Hemingway, Selected Letters, 1917–1961* (New York: Charles Scribner's Sons, 1981), 276.
93. The 1931 Cuba census (September 21, 1931); the twelfth national population census held in the Republic of Cuba indicated a total population of 3,962,344—an overall increase of 1,073,340 people, 2.61 percent over the 1919 census figure.

3. In the Author's Footsteps, Route One: From Whitehead Street West

94. According to the Monroe County Sheriff's Office (January 2020): in total, the crime rate dropped almost 14 percent from 2018 to 2019. Burglaries fell from 110 in 2018 to 86 the next year, according to the sheriff's office. Larceny crimes, which include theft, shoplifting, car break-ins and stolen bicycles, fell from 689 to 557.

95. This is a style of Romanesque Revival architecture named after the architect Henry Hobson Richardson (1838–1886).

96. The house was designed in 1889 by Scott, McDermott & Higgs, a local architectural firm.

97. By this date, Hemingway had numerous contacts inside the base, including the Thompson family. As the author's fame grew, he often invited certain guests to join him on fishing trips—the excursions a quid pro quo for the *Pilar*'s use of the submarine pen.

98. The couples' grave is located in located in lot 30, section C.

99. The Navy Field Arena often drew over five hundred fight fans. Hemingway also refereed at the venue on occasion, including on March 19, 1936.

100. Some boxing weight classes appear inside parenthesis.

101. One of the founders of Tifton, Georgia.

102. It is hard to believe today, but when the Hemingway family lived at the home, the other side of Whitehead Street was vacant except for the lighthouse property. Following World War II, the government built low-income housing; the source of the bricks used for the wall around the property also created a controversy.

103. His play *The Fifth Column* and numerous short stories, including "The Short Happy Life of Francis Macomber" and "The Snows of Kilimanjaro," both published in 1936.

104. Following the author's death, the boat was given to Gregorio Fuentes. Later, Castro's government seized *Pilar*.

105. Sources may vary.

106. The Big Island of Hawaii is farther south than Key West.

107. The land around the fort includes an attractive stretch of beach believed to bring the property total to eighty-seven acres. The fort's land that is closer to downtown Key West became part of the Truman Annex to Naval Air Station Key West.

4. In the Author's Footsteps, Route Two: Duval Street—Between Whitehead Street and White Street

108. Duval Street was named after William Pope Duval, the first territorial governor of Florida.

109. It is hard not to notice that the establishment was built around a tree. Legend has it that tree once served as the town's gallows.

110. Aquilino's World War I draft registration states his date of birth as December 20, 1886.

111. Hemingway was invited to participate in the inaugural ceremonies in Washington on January 19 and 20, 1961. His health made it impossible for him to attend.

112. The first formal library on the island was formed by an association in 1892. However, there was evidence that one existed prior to this date.

113. Rhoda Baker's Electric Kitchen was at this address in the 1930s, and Flaming Maggie's Fine Gay and Lesbian Bookstore occupied the spot in the 1980s and 1990s. At the time of this writing, SALT Gallery was located at 830 Fleming Street.

114. See City of Key West Florida, General ordinances/Chapter 22–Cemeteries, available at library.municode.com.

115. The 1846 hurricane destroyed the previous burial ground, which was located near Higgs Beach.

116. Ernest Hemingway wasn't a devout Catholic; however, he did pray at the Basilica of St. Mary Star of the Sea.

117. On October 6, 1908, the Louise Maloney Hospital, named in honor of his wife, opened its doors. Upon Dr. Maloney's death in 1916, the hospital was renamed the John B. Maloney Memorial Hospital.

118. Take Simonton Street south, then make a left turn on South Street (A1A). Stay on South Street until you reach Reynolds Street (four blocks). Make a right turn onto Reynolds Street and follow it south for three blocks until you reach your destination.

119. "Modern Hotel at Key West Opened by East Coast Co.," *Lakeland Evening Telegram*, January 1, 1921, 1.

120. Grace Hemingway, Ernest's mother, stayed in the hotel as well.

121. Thomas Albury Thompson and Mary Moon Symonett (1864–1956) were married on March 22, 1882.

5. In the Author's Footsteps, Route Three: Assorted Locations—From White Street East

122. In 1947, the structures were declared surplus by the U.S. Army and sold to Monroe County, which later leased East Martello to the Key West Art & Historical Society and West Martello to the Key West Garden Club.

6. The Key West Written Work of Ernest Hemingway, 1928–1940

123. The sales have been estimated at about sixty thousand by year's end.
124. House of Books Ltd. also issued a limited edition (three hundred copies, five pages) of *God Rest You Merry, Gentlemen*.
125. For an interesting local perspective, see "Ernest Hemingway's New Book One of Best in Literature Offerings," *Key West Citizen*, October 6, 1932, 3.
126. The short story was preparing his readers for the profanity that would be found in *The Green Hills of Africa*.
127. Hemingway did contribute a short story ("The Man with the Tyrolese Hat") to the periodical *Querschnitt* that was printed in June.
128. Harry Morgan was introduced as a character in a short story Hemingway called "One Trip Across." It was published by *Cosmopolitan* back in 1934.
129. Falange is defined as the Spanish Fascist movement that merged with traditional right-wing elements in 1937 to form the ruling party, the Falange Española Tradicionalista, under General Franco. It was formally abolished in 1977. The first issue of the book, with FAI (Federación Anarquista Ibérica) banner endpapers, is scarce—believed to be produced with one thousand numbered copies.
130. With an initial printing estimated at 75,000 copies, sales of the work would approach 200,000 copies by the end of the year.

7. From Souvenirs to Treasures

131. Thankfully, a number of valuable bibliographical guides exist and are suggested reading to anyone serious about collecting the author's work. *A Hemingway Check List*, by Lee Samuels, published by Charles Scribner's Sons in 1951, is another great place to start if you can find a copy.

132. Keep in mind that *The Torrents of Spring*, *The Sun Also Rises* and *A Farewell to Arms* were published prior to 1930.

133. Some books/films were made into television series, including *A Farewell to Arms* and *For Whom the Bell Tolls*. Remakes, theater productions or films based on short stories were also common.

134. The type of writing material used, be it pencil or ink, along with the stationery or letterhead used, will also impact value.

135. Copyright prohibits this author from printing samples of his handwriting or even unpublished letters.

136. The author's request No. 379034 was processed on November 19, 1993.

137. R.G. Leddy, Ernest Hemingway, letter, F.B.I. file, October 8, 1942, F.B.I. FOA request #379034.

138. D.M. Ladd, Ernest Hemingway, letter, F.B.I. file, April 27, 1943, F.B.I. FOA request #379034.

139. Redacted, Ernest Hemingway, letter, F.B.I. file, September 21, 1943, F.B.I. FOA request #379034.

140. Redacted, Ernest Hemingway, Edward "Ted" Scott, Foreign Miscellaneous, letter, F.B.I. file, September 1, 1954, F.B.I. FOA request #379034.

141. As do the over twenty photographs by Karsh that appeared on the cover of *LIFE* magazine.

8. The Hemingway Mythos

142. A must-read for every follower of the author is *Ernest Hemingway Selected Letters, 1917–1961*, edited by Carlos Baker and published by Scribner's Sons in 1981.

BIBLIOGRAPHY

Books

Baker, Carlos. *Ernest Hemingway: A Life Story*. New York: Charles Scribner's Sons, 1969.

———. *Ernest Hemingway Selected Letters 1917–1961*. New York: Charles Scribner's Sons, 1981.

———. *Hemingway, The Writer as Artist*. Princeton: Princeton University Press, 1963.

Baker, Mark Allen. *Between the Ropes at Madison Square Garden: The History of an Iconic Boxing Ring, 1925–2007*. Jefferson, NC: McFarland & Company, 2019.

———. *Title Town USA: Boxing in Upstate New York*. Charleston, SC: The History Press, 2019.

———. *The World Colored Heavyweight Championship, 1876–1937 (Drawing the Color Line)*. Jefferson, NC: McFarland & Company, 2020.

Dos Passos, John. *The Best Times*. New York: Signet, 1966.

Hanneman, Audre. *Ernest Hemingway, A Comprehensive Bibliography*. Princeton, NJ: Princeton University Press, 1967.

Hemingway, Ernest. *Death in the Afternoon*. New York: Charles Scribner's Sons, 1932.

———. *A Farewell to Arms*. New York: Charles Scribner's Sons, 1929.

———. *For Whom the Bell Tolls*. New York: Charles Scribner's Sons, 1940.

———. *In Our Time*. New York: Boni and Liveright, 1925.

————. *Men Without Women*. New York: Charles Scribner's Sons, 1927.

————. *The Fifth Column and the First Forty-Nine Stories*. New York: Charles Scribner's Sons, 1938.

————. *The Green Hills of Africa*. New York: Charles Scribner's Sons, 1935.

————. *The Old Man and the Sea*. New York: Charles Scribner's Sons, 1952.

————. *The Spanish Earth*. Cleveland: The J.B. Savage Company, 1938.

————. *The Sun Also Rises*. New York: Charles Scribner's Sons, 1926.

————. *Three Stories and Ten Poems*. Paris: Robert McAlmon (Contact Publishing Company), 1923.

————. *To Have and Have Not*. New York: Charles Scribner's Sons, 1927.

————. *The Torrents of Spring*. New York: Charles Scribner's Sons, 1926.

————. *Winner Take Nothing*. New York: Charles Scribner's Sons, 1933.

Hemingway, Leicester. *My Brother, Ernest Hemingway*. Miami, FL: Winchester House Publishers, 1980.

Hotchner, A.E. *Papa Hemingway*. New York: Random House, 1966.

Key West in Transition: A Guide Book for Tourists. Key West, FL: Key West Authority, 1934.

McLendon, James. *Papa Hemingway in Key West*. Key West, FL: Langley Press, 1984.

Meyers, Jeffrey. *Hemingway, A Biography*, New York: Harper and Row, 1985.

Polk's Key West City Directory, 1927–1928. Jacksonville, FL: R.L. Polk & Company, 1927.

Ross, Lillian. *Portrait of Hemingway*. New York: Simon and Schuster, 1961.

Wells, Sharon. *Sloppy Joe's Bar, The First Fifty Years*. Key West, FL: Key West Saloon, 1983.

Young, Philip. *Ernest Hemingway: A Reconsideration*. University Park: Pennsylvania State University Press, 1966.

Brochures and Programs

1994 Hemingway Days Festival, Key West

Internet Sites

ancestry.com
billiongraves.com
biography.com

boxrec.com
brittanica.com
chroniclingamerica.loc.gov
findagrave.com
finebooksmagazine.com
friendsofthekeywestcemetery.com
hemingwayhome.com
keywesttravelguide.com
newspapers.com
wikipedia.com
youtube.com

Interviews

Kermit "Shine" Forbes and James "Iron Baby" Roberts, 1994 Hemingway
    Days Festival, Key West, Florida

Legal Documents

United States Department of Justice, Federal Bureau of Investigation

Magazines

Atlantic Monthly
The Boulevardier
Collier's
Cosmopolitan
Esquire
Exile
Fact
Fortune
Holiday
Ken
Library Journal
LIFE

Little Review
Look
New Masses
New Republic
New Yorker
Saturday Review
Scribner's Magazine
This Quarter
Transatlantic Review
Transition
True
Verve
Vogue

Newspapers

Baltimore (MD) Sun
Bismarck (ND) Tribune
Brownsville (TX) Herald
Chapel Hill (NC) Weekly
Chicago (IL) Daily Tribune
Daily Independent (Elizabeth City, NC)
Daily Worker (Chicago, IL)
Evening Star (Washington, D.C.)
Evening World (New York, NY)
Henderson (NC) Daily Dispatch
Imperial Valley Press (El Centro, CA)
Indianapolis (IN) Times
Key Outpost (Key West, FL)
Key West (FL) Citizen
Key West (FL) Morning Journal
Lakeland (FL) Evening Telegram
Lexington (MS) Advertiser
Miami (FL) Herald
Miami (FL) Times
Montana Labor News (Butte, MT)
Morgan County Democrat (McConnelsville, OH)

New York (NY) Times
Omaha (NE) Guide
Red Lodge (MT) Daily News
Toronto Star (Toronto, CA)
Waterbury (CT) Democrat

Organizations—Research

Associated Press
Bureau of Labor Statistics' Consumer Price Index (CPI)
The Smithsonian Institution
United Press International
United States Census Bureau

Photographs and Archival Sources

John F. Kennedy Presidential Library and Museum, Boston
State Archives of Florida
The Library of Congress
The National Archives and Records Administration
United States Department of State – Bureau of Consular Affairs

Trademarks

Captain Tony's Saloon, DECCA, RCA Victor, Penguin Books, Bantam Books, Scribner's, Sloppy Joe's, Strand and Warner Brothers Pictures are registered trademarks.

ABOUT THE AUTHOR

Mark Allen Baker is an author of over twenty-five nonfiction books. As a Hemingway historian and connoisseur, he spoke at the 1994 Hemingway Days Festival in Key West. Baker is the only person to serve the International Boxing Hall of Fame as an author, historian, chairperson, sponsor, volunteer and biographer. He also sits on the Board of Directors for the Connecticut Boxing Hall of Fame. He lives in Hebron, Connecticut, and Lakewood Ranch, Florida. For additional information, or to contact the author, please see readmarkallenbaker.com.

Remember, help is always available at the National Suicide Prevention Lifeline: 800-273-8255.